Working with the community

A Guide to Corporate Social Responsibility

David Clutterbuck and Deborah Snow

Weidenfeld and Nicolson · London
Published in association with Kingfisher plc

Published in Great Britain by
George Weidenfeld & Nicolson Limited
91 Clapham High Street
London SW4 7TA

ISBN 0 297 81177 0

Printed in Great Britain by
Butler & Tanner Ltd.,
Frome and London

Contents

'It is a prime responsibility of managements to ensure that their companies are good corporate citizens, caring not just for those with a direct stake in the business – shareholders, employers, customers, suppliers – but for the general public and the environment in the broadest sense of the term.

The domestic and international reputation of UK industry and commerce depends on the conduct of businesses of all kinds, large and small, and Kingfisher is to be commended for making this Guide to Corporate Social Responsibility available to all.

Social responsibility encompasses many different aspects of business life. It means putting customers first, and providing them with good, safe and reliable products and services. It means being a first-class employer, providing fair pay, good conditions and decent pensions for employees. It involves genuine concern for health and safety, and a commitment to good employee involvement and communications.

Every firm has a responsibility to its suppliers, which, at its most basic, means paying bills on time. But good relations go much further. Many firms today take a partnership approach to their sourcing decisions. This involves working closely with suppliers, encouraging them to produce to exacting standards, and, where necessary, helping them to do so.

Companies with a sense of social responsibility ensure that in all their operations they are 'good neighbours', ensuring strict control of noise, emissions and waste. In the broader sense, good corporate citizenship means involvement in business schemes for inner city renewal, building links with local schools, helping to train the long-term unemployed, and creating jobs for the disadvantaged. This is vital if the emergence of an urban underclass in our inner cities is to be prevented.

Corporate social responsibility is not charity. It is enlightened self interest. It is also a moral imperative in my view. There can be very few better reasons for hoping that this guide will have the wide readership it deserves.'

John Banham
Director General
Confederation of British Industry

Foreword

Like many other companies in Britain and elsewhere, Kingfisher has progressively formalised its policies, procedures and behaviours towards the communities in which it does business. This has not been a sudden revelation – the various companies which make up our Group have a strong history of community involvement and awareness of social responsibility issues. Rather, it has come from the gradual recognition that any organization concerned to maintain a relationship of trust with its employees and customers has no option but to develop consistent and thoughtful approaches to these issues.

Like many other companies, we have learned that a healthy business depends upon a healthy community; and that our involvement in community affairs should no longer be regarded as charitable giving, but as a partnership for mutual benefit.

In preparing this guide, Kingfisher is not setting itself up to be a paragon of business virtue. Rather, our aim is to help other companies travel along a path where we ourselves are still near the start of our journey. Indeed, the pace at which new social and environmental issues emerge means that we have constantly to re-examine aspects of our business against changing perceptions of what constitutes best behaviour. ('Acceptable' behaviour is often not enough.)

We have welcomed the opportunity to learn from other companies – some of whose experience is represented in the chapters that follow – how they establish and maintain high standards of social responsibility across diverse and geographically spread organizations. We do hope other companies will find this information useful. We, ourselves, intend to continue learning, from other companies, from our customers and from our staff.

Geoffrey Mulcahy
Chairman and Chief Executive
Kingfisher plc

Introduction

This management guide has been prepared under the sponsorship of Kingfisher plc to pull together the multiple strands that form corporate social responsibility. Our aim has been to provide a framework for developing a coherent, company-wide approach to social responsibility issues; to provide examples of best practice; and to provide checklists that will help the concerned company assess where it is now.

We have not covered *every* aspect of corporate social responsibility – there are far too many, with more emerging continuously. Rather, we have concentrated on the main themes and illustrated each with specific areas of activity. There are no perfect companies, just as there are no perfect people – but every company owes it to its stakeholders to strive to achieve demonstrably high social responsibility performance.

For shareholders, it helps raise the value of their investment – not least because companies that are sensitive to their environment tend to be better and faster at perceiving and taking advantage of social and market change.

For employees, it helps increase the sense of pride in their jobs – most people prefer to work for an organization with a high reputation, rather than for one with a poor or neutral reputation.

To customers and suppliers, it helps provide confidence that this is a good business to do business with. This has a substantial impact in maintaining customer loyalty – a key factor in achieving superior returns for almost all businesses.

In its dealings with the community in general, the socially responsible, involved company will frequently find that it has better relationships with local and national legislators and bureaucrats; and greater opportunities to influence the environment, in which it trades.

A decade ago, most companies would have regarded these as intangible, indirect benefits. Now these issues are increasingly being seen as central to the business organization's well-being.

This guide is intended to be of help and value both to companies

which already have strong established social responsibility programmes, and those which are just starting out.

Our survey (see page 170) indicates that many companies do
not consciously exchange information on best social responsibility
practice. We hope that the ideas in the following pages will
encourage them to do so.

David Clutterbuck and Deborah Snow   July 1990

1 Responsibility towards customers

On the face of it, behaving responsibly towards the customer is the most obvious area of self-interest for commercial organizations. Public sector organizations, too, will normally have their objectives written in terms of fulfilling specific customer needs. Certainly, there is considerable evidence – for example, from PIMS data – to suggest that organizations which are truly customer-focused tend on average to have returns on investment as much as six times that of companies which are not. And, certainly, many more companies are now recognising that the value of a customer lies not in a one-off sale, but in ensuring he or she comes back again and again and again.

The aim, put simply, must be to be seen as 'a good business to do business with'. In practice, such a public perception is only sustainable if the company goes to very considerable lengths to ensure that it is supported by reality. Once it has gained this kind of reputation, the company has to continue to work hard to ensure that it is not undermined by contrary behaviours.

The customer element of a social responsibility agenda will therefore consist of:

- customer responsiveness
- provision of information
- product safety
- ethical marketing.

1.1 Customer responsiveness

Thundered the *Financial Times* in February 1990: 'Successful shops will be those which give the shoppers what they want in terms of what products they want, at the price they are prepared to pay, in the surroundings they find convenient. Like many things which seems obvious, these ideas are too often missed by those involved.' Much the same applies for any business. The key to delivering what the customer wants lies in:

- having systems to listen to customers

• having systems to make sure that necessary improvements happen.

There are three main times when a company comes into contact with the customer:
– at the point of sale
– for servicing
– when it receives complaints

Astute companies are increasingly dedicating significant resources to training people at the first two points.

They are running training courses on answering the phone, product knowledge and general interaction techniques. In addition they are publishing customer guides, giving detailed information on how to use the product and what to do if it goes wrong.

They are also finding, however, that this is not enough. The vast majority of failures to meet customer's needs arise because of systems, standards or structures outside of the control of the people at the front line – i.e. most problems are management problems. Customer service programmes that work are those which recognise that the management issues need to be tackled first, or at least in parallel with the general smile training.

As for complaints, companies should ensure:
– there is one clear address for all product complaints and queries. People need to know exactly who to call or write to. Ideally, this information should be on the product itself, rather than in operating literature that can be lost or destroyed.

For service operations, however, the complaint should be dealt with at the point of delivery. Compare the following experiences:

• A large financial institution directed complaints to head office. The department responsible grew to the extent that, at over 100 people, it was no longer possible to accommodate it in the building. Meanwhile, line managers failed to put complaints right, because they understandably felt that that was now a head office function.

• Avis calculated the cost of dealing with complaints centrally and found that the extra paperwork, loss of time and other indirect costs came on average to more than £20. Added to this was the frustration of the customer at the desk, who has to wait days for his or her problem to be sorted out. Now Avis encourages its desk staff to resolve customer problems, up to the £20 level, entirely on their own authority.

– queries are turned around rapidly. Ideally, written complaints should be acknowledged by return – preferably with a telephone call. Every hour's delay allows the customer to grow more frustrated and to tell more people.
– there are technical experts within the company who will investigate complaints with the customer.
– there is a director with responsibility for ensuring that complaints are

- handled properly
- analysed for trends
- brought up for discussion at board meetings

A handful of companies has also experimented with rotating responsibility among the top team, a month at a time, for answering all complaints that arrive by letter or telephone.
– they check out whether customer is satisfied with the actions taken to put his or her problem right. Some companies have also appointed an ombudsman to represent the interests of the customers who are dissatisfied with how their complaint has been handled.
– that people at all levels in the organization realise how valuable complaints are in identifying areas for improvement. By constantly taking notice of complaints, companies can achieve competitive advantage, simply by becoming better at the operational activities that affect customers.

So valuable does Corning Glass in the United States regard complaints, that it produced a booklet for customers, guiding them on how to complain.

Companies in the food manufacturing industry, which have experienced sympathetic complaints experts on call, have found that in the recent spate of queries about food hygiene and product safety, these travelling troubleshooters have more than earned their keep. The sight of a company employee on their doorstep to sort out the problem convinces customers that the company really cares.

If customers believe that the company, or at least someone in it, is on their side, their goodwill towards it and their confidence in its products will rise.

Although effective complaints handling creates customer goodwill, ideally companies will identify most problem areas – and opportunities to improve products and service – by actively asking for customers' opinions. Normal market research techniques, such as opinion polling and mystery shoppers, can provide some useful information. But many companies are finding greater value from approaching customers direct, either inviting them in to talk about their problems and needs, or sending employees out to find out for themselves.

Case study: *Wessex Water plc*

Wessex Water provides public information on policy matters and about individual schemes. During 1989 it held open days, exhibitions and lectures, and provided pamphlets and school materials on a wide variety of subjects.

Customers' interests are represented via liaison and consultative committees. New customer services committees were proposed in the Water Act and the new company plans to retain a local dialogue with the community it serves.

It also holds frequent meetings with organizations such as the Confederation of British Industry, the National Farmers Union and the Country landowners Association to ensure that their interests are considered.

Case study: *Safeway plc*

Safeway part of the Argyll Group, has taken a strategic decision to achieve differentiation from other food retailers by developing a reputation as the most responsive to customer needs, both nationally and at store level.

Every week, the directors visit about seven stores and look at them through the customers' eyes. They note details such as signage, product ranges and the amount of car parking space available.

When a store opened at St Helens, Merseyside, in July 1989, the company set up a customer suggestion scheme inviting customers to comment on its supermarket and to offer suggestions on how to improve it. The scheme was so successful that it has been extended to 14 other stores from Penzance in Cornwall to Irvine in Scotland. The St Helens branch then took the scheme a step further by organizing a customer conference. 100 people were selected from more than 1000 who had sent in comments at St Helens. The participants spent the day grilling Safeway executives. Many of their suggestions have already been put into action. For example, the store used customer complaints about a dangerous exit to put pressure on local planning authorities to permit a second exit from its car park and to install a pelican crossing. It has also changed trolley designs because many customers complained the handle was too high, making it difficult to pick things out of the trolley.

Case study: *British Gas plc*

British Gas has published a guide entitled, 'Commitment to our customers', laying down the standards and quality of service customers can expect. Customer relations managers are being appointed, who have the authority to award compensation payments up to £5,000 and to deal with any outstanding customer problems.

Case study: *Woolworths*

In July 1987, Woolworths introduced an 'excellence' training programme. This aims to make sales assistants fully proficient and more confident when dealing with customers. The programme rewards staff for their achievements and for their progress towards standards of personal and team excellence, and is part of the company's £5.5 million annual training investment.

Case study: *Kwik Fit*

For Kwik Fit, one of Britain's leading car servicing and repair companies, safety comes from good workmanship and extensive guarantees.

When cars are brought in for repairs, customers expect that to be the end of their problem. Kwik Fit goes to remarkable lengths to make sure that this is the case. It does so by
● training every member of staff so that they know exactly what to do, before they are allowed to work on customers' vehicles and by insisting on frequent refresher training
● showing the customer what is to be done before the job is started, and what has actually been done when the job is finished
● offering guarantees over and above those from the manufacturers
● publishing its own Code of Practice, which is monitored both by internal auditors and by independent organizations.

Checklist
1. Does your company have effective systems for listening to its customers?
2. Does it have a customer champion and/or ombudsman?
3. Are complaints regarded as a problem or an opportunity?
4. Does your company measure and analyse all complaints and use them to improve products and services?

1.2 Provision of information

Over the past decade there has been a growing expectation among consumers for accurate, relevant information about the products and services they buy. In part, this arises from a desire for reassurance; in part because people who want to make informed choices need information.

Case study: *Tesco plc*

Tesco has been at the forefront of nutritional labelling on its products. Customers can pick up a selection of free booklets from Tesco's branches covering topics such as fat, salt, fitness and health, vitamins and minerals.

In addition, the company publishes a cheap booklet on nutrition to help the customer understand its products.

Case study: *Safeway plc*

Safeway publishes a series of booklets on nutrition. The Safeway Nutrition Advice Service is a department set up to extend the company's customer service. It aims to ensure that Safeway products comply with the highest dietary standards.

The service is responsible for ensuring that products carry nutrition information. Eventually, all Safeway food will carry this information, in addition to the list of ingredients, which are required by law.

Customers can contact the advice service to help with any diet, nutrition and health queries and for further nutritional information on health products.

Safeway, voted the 'greenest supermarket' in 'The Green Consumer's Supermarket Shopping Guide' by John Elkington and Julia Hailes, also gave out free 'green action' calendars in late 1989. The calendars highlight different environmental issues each month, giving practical advice on how everyone in a family can help tackle environmental problems. Solutions ranged from building a bird table, through converting the car to lead free petrol to using bottle banks.

Checklist
1. Does your company have a programme to identify what information customers require and to ensure they receive it?

1.3 Product safety

The legal requirements upon companies to ensure the safety of their products are becoming tighter and tighter. Debate within the European Commission as to how – and how far – to extend product liability has been heated and is likely eventually to require manufacturers to demonstrate more rigorous preventive systems and to raise the level of penalties for failing to react sufficiently rapidly to real or potential problems.

Customers, too, are becoming more demanding in terms of product safety. Reaction to food safety problems of listeria in eggs and soft cheeses, and to BSE in beef demonstrates that the *perception* of risk is enough to persuade people to exercise the power of negative choice.

Companies wishing to keep ahead of the legal requirements and to reduce the risk of customer distrust of their products should ensure they have:
* a monitoring system to give early warning of real or potential problems and to bring them to top management attention
* formal and informal contacts with organizations representing consumers
* a network of experts, who can be trusted to give a truly impartial analysis of any problems (rather than give the answer they think the company wants). Ideally, any potentially serious problems should be put out to several organizations, to ensure a representative spread of expert opinions.
* a system for rapid response – e.g. to remove suspect stock from the shelves. Wherever possible, those systems should be tested from time to time with a 'product fire drill' to make sure they work in practice.

Case study: *ICI Group*

ICI states that it is determined to encourage the responsible use of its agrochemicals. The aim is to maximize their effectiveness while minimising the risks inherent in their use.

ICI's Product Stewardship Campaign is one example of this intent in action. The Product Stewardship programme looks at every step from manufacture through marketing and distribution, to final use and impact on the environment.

The risks are not always the obvious ones, says ICI in its annual reprt for 1989.

For example, some years ago ICI discovered that its leading herbicide could be mistaken for cola or coffee. The risks were increased because farmers, in the Third World especially, sometimes stored leftovers in old bottles against the advice on the label. The company immediately changed the colour of the product and added an unpleasant-smelling agent.

7

In Malaysia, ICI uses posters, radio advertising, training sessions and videos to teach good practice to dealers, smallholders and estate managers. It also spends time designing clear, informative lables to ensure that distributors and users understand each product and its related dangers.

Checklist
1. Does your company seek to more than meet the legal requirements for product safety?
2. Does it have systems to provide early warning of possible safety hazards?
3. Does it have a disaster plan, to withdraw a suspect product rapidly?

1.4 Ethical marketing

The Advertising Standards Authority regularly has to deal with companies that have misinformed the public. Its case report for June 1990, for example, adjudicates on a double glazing advertiser, which illustrated leaded glass windows, but quoted a price which did not apply to leaded glass.

Says the report: 'This is a technique which understandably irritates most of us. More important, it fails to meet basic standards of straight-forward information, which readers have a right to expect from such advertising. It is unrealistic to list all prices, and every detail for every type of product, but if any prices are quoted they must not mislead.'

Every month the authority has to deal with hundreds of complaints referred by the public about advertising by companies ranging from large multinationals to small local concerns.

The range of complaints extends from dubious to taste to deliberate deception. Common problems currently include false environmental claims and sales promotions which do not mention important conditions attached.

Most of the companies involved could have saved themselves embarrassment by contacting the ASA in advance.

The issue of green advertising illustrates how marketing enthusiasm can undermine ethical marketing practices. To quote the *Financial Times* in June 1990: 'Green advertising is challenging. The arguments are often more abstract or bogged down by complex scientific issues. It is arguably easier to seduce someone into buying something with an image of ostentatious opulence, than with an intricate explanation of how a disposable nappy manufacturer has eradicated dioxins from the pulp production process.'

Some large companies came under severe attack for their cynicism. People aren't green about green issues and the *Financial Times* goes on to record:

'Saatchi's research shows that people now expect companies to be environmentally aware in every area of their activities. Companies cannot expect people to be impressed by their new green products or by their advertisements – if they do not take a responsible attitude to the environment in areas such as corporate strategy and production planning.'

In August 1989, the government announced that it would introduce a voluntary 'green label' system by the end of 1991. Companies will be able to use it as an official logo on their products if they can demonstrate they have achieved a significant reduction in the burden a product places on the environment. The scheme will look at the environmental impact from 'cradle to grave' – from the original raw materials, produced through forestry, agriculture or mining, through its life cycle, to how it is disposed.

Case study: *Friends of the Earth and the 'green con'*

The international pressure group, Friends of the Earth, has been at the forefront of the campaign to change companies' environmental behaviour.

According to Pippa Hyam, senior information officer, the green revolution started in earnest after the widespread deaths of North Sea seals from an unknown disease. She said: 'It is at this point that the wider media such as *The Sun*, the *Daily Mirror* and *Today* started to cover environmental issues on a regular basis. A Mori opinion poll taken in May 1988 showed that only 18% of the population had ever bought a 'green' product. By May 1989, this had risen to 41%.'

But as companies struggled to compete for this affluent and growing slice of the market, a disturbing trend towards inaccurate labelling became apparent.

Reputable organisations started to make banal claims about their cars. A 1989 advert for a popular family car claimed;

'(This car) is capable of running on unleaded petrol. This means it's as ozone friendly as it is economical.'

As Neil Verlander, information officer at FoE, explains: 'The statement was ridiculous since lead is too heavy to reach the stratosphere and doesn't interfere with the composition of the earth's ozone layer. There is no connection, therefore, between the use of unleaded petrol and damage to the ozone layer.'

This company wasn't the only one to jump on the green band wagon, so in late 1989 Friends of the Earth started to collect examples of blatant eco-hypocrisy and later presented a number of companies with a Green Con Award.

Pippa explains: 'Slogans were conjured up, confusing the public. Companies were trying to market their products as 'green' without actually changing the product. The aim of the awards was to make companies aware that if they persisted in using such marketing techniques they would be caught out.' More than 280 nominations were received.

One of the main complaints of those who wrote in with nominations was that a large number of companies are keen to present a green image to the public, even though their business activities are environmentally harmful. Another concern was that green products were subject to mark up, with no guarantee that higher prices reflected genuine extra production costs.

A report by the Advertising Standards Authority in July 1989 warned those attracted to the language and images of greenery: 'Some advertisers appear to be paying more attention to making sure that their wares are perceived as sitting on the green side of the fence than to checking the factual accuracy of their claims and thereby maintaining the truthfulness of their advertising.'

The aerosol industry came under particular attack. Some companies had labelled their products ozone friendly when in fact they still contained chemicals to damage the ozone layer. The response of companies, which had been nominated for the awards, varied, but most responded positively. One company received the Green Con Award for labelling spot remover with the statement 'Contains no propellant alleged to damage the ozone,' when in fact it did. The company agreed to remove the product from the shelves within three months unless alternatives could be found.

Another company labelled its cleaner for footwear and belts as ozone friendly. It agreed to cover the label on the cans until new ones came through.

The motor industry received a large number of nominations. Many car companies had already moved towards the introduction of unleaded petrol and 3-way catalytic converters, but they were often tempted to oversell what was already a big selling point. Two companies even claimed that carbon dioxide produced by their catalytic converters was harmless. Carbon dioxide is the biggest contributor to the Greenhouse effect. More than 16 per cent of carbon dioxide emissions in the UK are from cars.

More people are anxious to use their purchasing power to help protect the environment, either by not buying a product or by buying a particular brand that is less environmentally damaging than its competitors.

In a free market, companies must give the consumer the necessary information to make environmentally sound choices.

With this in mind, Friends of the Earth is now pressing for product labelling that would take account of the full environmental impact of a product 'from cradle to grave' including energy use, pollution and waste associated with raw materials' extraction and use, manufacture, packaging, product use and disposal. In the long term this would include a legal obligation for products to carry environmental impact statements.

Checklist
1. Does your company have someone responsible for monitoring marketing practice on ethical and fair practice grounds?

2 Responsibilities towards employees

One of the emergent issues of the late 1980s and early 1990s is the importance of public perception as a factor in people's choice of employer. It has become increasingly clear that would-be employees, especially those with scarce skills, place a significant value on the reputation of an employer, on two counts: how it behaves towards the world at large (i.e. is it a quality organisation, which cares for the community?); and how it treats its employees.

These issues affect not only recruitment but how people perform at work, how long they stay and how they speak and behave as ambassadors for the company (an important marketing issue). The cost implications of being seen as a poor or indifferent employer can therefore be very considerable. IBM, for example, calculates that it costs £150,000 to replace a qualified engineer; A northern manufacturing company calculates the cost of losing a graduate trainee after two years at around £50,000. Both of these companies have good retention rates; yet both are concerned to increase retention by paying more attention to meeting people's needs for development and job satisfaction.

To a considerable extent, this area of social responsibility has been covered by legislation – for example, on equal opportunities, employee rights regarding dismissal, or on health and safety. European legislation will gradually add to what is already a substantial legislative burden. But legislation generally represents only the minimum of action required in any area; moreover, some legislation, such as requirements for companies with more than 20 people to employ a minimum of 3% disabled, has been largely ignored, even by government departments and agencies. Similarly, equal opportunities legislation has had little impact on the promotion of more women into middle and senior management.

It makes sense, therefore, for the socially responsible company to ask itself:

Checklist
1. Are we sure we are aware of, and have policies concerning all the issues likely to affect our reputation as a responsible, caring employer?
2. Are we meeting the legal requirements in full, in spirit as well as to the letter?
3. Do we significantly exceed those requirements?
4. Do our employees perceive the company as a caring employer?

To cover all the relevant issues here would require a book (or two) of its own. We have therefore focused on some of the most critical issues:
• equal opportunities
• developing talent
• health and safety
• employee welfare
• managing dissent.

2.1 Equal opportunities

Discrimination at work affects a wide variety of minorities. If experience in the United States is anything to go by, companies will eventually be obliged to take note of the special circumstances of the over-45s, the obese, homosexuals and even the plain ugly. UK legislation, however, has tended to focus on four main areas of discrimination – racial, sexual, religious and disability. For the most part, legislation is national in scope, but some regulations are regional in their application – for example, recent employment regulations in Northern Ireland are designed to ensure that programmes of positive discrimination in hiring are not decimated by last-in, first-out redundancy policies.

There is no general body for enforcing equal opportunities in the UK. The Equal Opportunities Commission, set up in 1975, handles women's issues, the Commission for Racial Equality deals with race and the disabled have to make do with a set of voluntary bodies, whose task is to make sure they get a fair hearing in the workplace.

Despite a spate of equal opportunities legislation, employers are continuing to discriminate against women, the disabled and ethnic minorities, according to the TUC, the Equal Opportunities Commission and organizations, such as the Spastics Society, which represent the disabled. All of these organizations are advocating affirmative action programmes to combat discrimination.

These should be based around a detailed and comprehensive equal opportunities policy and programme.

In theory, predicted shortages of entrants should have stimulated companies to greater efforts, to ensure that they recruit from minority groups, pay them at the same rates, and promote representative proportions of those minorities into supervisory and management positions. Certainly, there are a number of well-publicized examples of companies that have done so. For example, several retailers have announced programmes of positive discrimination in favour of over-45s; others have deliberately located new factories in inner city areas with high black unemployment. But evidence that companies in general have increased activity in this area is rather more difficult to find.

What evidence there is, from both sides of the Atlantic, suggests that equal opportunities will only be achieved if companies take the following steps:

1) Have a policy outlining the company's standpoint on this issue and clear goals to achieve.
2) Have an active programme to identify and encourage candidates for recruitment or promotion to come forward, and to help them overcome any disadvantages that reduce their eligibility. For example, when personnel staff from some companies visit inner city schools, they take with them black and Asian managers and apprentices, to create rapport with minority students, who feel less threatened and more encouraged to ask questions about opportunities within the company.
3) Measure current performance in a manner that allows progress to be monitored year on year. In practice, this requires the company to gather sensitive data about the people who work for it and to analyse carefully the proportions of key minorities in relation to the population as a whole and in relation to the spread of people at different levels in the organization. The very sensitivity of the data can make this a difficult task. Ingrained suspicion may make people question what the data is used for. Hence it is essential for the company to explain carefully how the information will be processed and that only anonymous statistics will be released. When the data is collated, it should be released as quickly as possible into the company newspaper to reassure people that the company's intentions are genuine. Where possible, it is also advisable to get people to fill in questionnaires about racial origins themselves. It increases their confidence in the programme and also causes far fewer errors.

Other rough and ready methods of establishing a company's equal opportunities performance include simply asking people whether they feel they are being discriminated against. In spite of the growing popularity of the attitude survey as a means of determining how employees view their work, their immediate boss and the company as a whole, it is scarcely ever used to ask employees how they view the treatment they receive as compared with the treatment of other workers around them. Yet what better way to detect discrimination than through the eyes and ears of the people who suffer it?

4) Be alert to unintentional discrimination. The classic case here – certainly the most frequently quoted – is the New York Police force, which insisted on a minimum height for applicants of 5 feet 10 inches. This discriminated not only against women but against Hispanics and Orientals, who are often smaller than the average Northern European male. Analysis of the job content showed that the only time height was required was to fire over the top of a car. Even then the person only had to be 5 feet 8 inches. The force reduced the height stipulation after a woman brought an action against it. The resultant publicity made organizations on both sides of the Atlantic look closely at their recruiting policy for unintentional discrimination.

In the following pages we have attempted to focus on some of the more innovative and socially responsible companies where positive discrimination has become a requirement. The principal groups these companies are tackling are racial minorities, the physically handicapped, women and the mature employee.

Checklist
1. Do you have a written code of practice on equal opportunities?
2. Is your equal opportunities policy led at board room level?
3. Do you have a senior manager responsible for monitoring and implementing equal opportunities?

2.1.1 *Ethnic minorities*

The industrial history of the British Isles is one of gradual assimilation of ethnic minorities. The beginnings of industrialization were fuelled by Huguenot immigrants, bringing new technologies of cloth making, and their absorption into society was not without heated discussion and antagonism. At the turn of the twentieth century, London and Liverpool were the focus for immigration of large numbers of Jews from Russia (many of them under the impression, initially, that they had landed in the United States). In the near-century since, Britain has also absorbed waves of Chinese, Cypriot, Caribbean, African and Asian immigration. The degree of discrimination – or a difficulty in becoming absorbed into working society – these immigrants experience depends on a variety of factors, of which the most important may be:

– the level of technical skill/education they hold
– the degree to which they are noticeably 'different' and determined to preserve their difference
– the scale of immigration
– the prevailing economic climate
– the homogeneity of the society which they are trying to enter.

Depending on these factors, a group may be fully assimilated immediately, at one extreme, or only after several generations, at the other.

The socially responsible employer will want to establish the demographics of the local labour pool; to understand the cultural background from which major ethnic minority groups come; and to recognise that the organization may need to adapt its requirements as much as it requires minority employees to change their behaviour to fit the established working culture. Only then can it construct viable programmes which will lead to fair representation at all levels in the organisation.

Checklist
1. Do you have a clear statement of policy on racial discrimination, and on objectives in equal opportunity hiring and promotion?
2. Have you communicated this to *all* employees? to the local community?
3. Do you know the ethnic composition of your workforce and the local community?
4. Do you have proactive measures to:
   attract higher percentages of ethnic minority job applicants
   help them qualify for recruitment
   promote ethnic minorities into junior and middle management positions?
5. Do you provide training for managers and other influencers in the organization, to reinforce non-discriminatory behaviour?
6. Have you reviewed all your recruitment and promotion practices to avoid unintentional racial bias?

Case study: *Ford Motor Co.*

Ford has one of the most comprehensive and thoroughly researched equal opportunities policies and initiatives in the country.

Ford has a joint statement on equal opportunity signed by the company and both sets of trade unions. The joint statement declares opposition to discrimination at work on the grounds of race, religious beliefs, creed, colour, nationality, ethnic or national origins, marital or parental status, sex, non-job related handicaps or age. It commits the company to the elimination of discrimination on these grounds, to the active promotion of equal opportunity and to the provision of training in equal opportunity practices for all employees.

To implement these policies, the company has an equal opportunities department which is based at Warley in Essex and headed by a senior manager, Ken Baker.

Baker was formerly plant manager at Dagenham, responsible for a workforce of 2,600, half of whom were minorities, so he has credibility with line management and a ground level understanding of the issues. He explains: 'We introduced our equal opportunities policy before it became law because it makes sound business sense to consider everybody in the workforce.'

The department's role is to develop and update the company's equal opportunity policy and strategy, to monitor and advise management on progress and trends, and to develop and assist in new initiatives. It is also responsible for reviewing opportunities within the community. The company has focussed its activities on positive action for ethnic minorities and women with special emphasis on educational assistance.

The company had a firm basis from which to work since it has been monitoring the ethnic background of its workforce since 1967 at its Dagenham plant. Figures at that time showed that 34.7 per cent of all job applicants for hourly paid jobs were from ethnic minorities and 32.5 per cent of these were hired.

At that time the personnel manager decided what 'colour' the applicant was.

A question on ethnic origins was included on a pilot basis in application forms for graduate vacancies in 1978 and 1979. This system of self classification was extended to all application forms soon after. Any applicant who does not answer the ethnic origin question is classified by his or her interviewer.

To implement an equal opportunities policy effectively, up-to-date information is vital. In an article in the Equal Opportunities Report, March 1989, John Hougham, Ford's executive personnel director points out that the cost of monitoring has not been high. The cost of recording the ethnic origins of over 10,000 new recruits and providing the computer statistics for all 70,000 employees was calculated in 1979 at around £1,000. This works out as less than 10p for each new recruit and 1.5p for each existing employee.

Ford also gathers information about local demographics, identifying for example that 20% of the population of nearby Newham comes from ethnic minority backgrounds. The equal opportunities department believes that the ratio between the ethnic minorities and white employees should be the same at each hourly and salary grade. In reality, ethnic minorities are concentrated far more in the lower grades, with the numbers tapering off as the skill level rises. At present, less than 3% are in the skilled grades. The proportion of ethnic minority technical trainees has risen from 1% in 1977 to 4.9% in 1988 and this should eventually be reflected among the trained workforce.

Baker and his team are determined to bring even more young black and coloured people onto their apprenticeship scheme. They discovered that ethnic minority candidates formed about 5% of apprenticeship applications yet only about 2% of the intake at Dagenham. This caused them to question whether the recruitment test introduced a cultural bias. It didn't, so the Technical Training Centre at Dagenham organized a careers conference for teachers, parents and careers advisors to discuss the problems of recruiting young Asians and blacks onto Ford training programmes.

As a result of the discussions, Ford took women and ethnic minority apprentices to local schools, so that prospective candidates could talk to somebody of their age and background about the training. In addition, the recruitment brochure was redesigned to include more pictures of young blacks, women and Asians. Staff awareness of the problem was raised by discussion and company courses. The equal opportunities department sent information sheets to schools describing the entrance test and giving practical examples so that pupils could prepare for it.

The proportion of blacks, Asians and coloureds among job applicants rose from 5% to 15% by 1988 thanks to these measures. But, explains Baker: 'Only two thirds of the applicants were acceptable. This was because in inner city areas, educational standards seem to be lower. Kids don't attend school, so they don't get the mathematical and technological background necessary to get onto the apprenticeship courses.'

So the team set about trying to help the youngsters through the test. The answer was a bridging scheme. Ford now pays £60,000 per annum for a year course at Newham College, East London, for about 15 youngsters between the ages of 16 and 18. The first course started in September 1988 and was attended by 12 boys from ethnic minority groups and two white girls. More than 50% of the students went on to join the Ford apprenticeship scheme. The company pays them a bursary for attendance, at a rate only slightly less than what the company pays undergraduates and the students are not committed to join Ford afterwards. The scheme proved so successful that a second class was started in 1989.

The equal opportunities department is also taking part in the Newham Compact, a government sponsored scheme to build up a partnership between youngsters, education and employers. Baker is on the steering committee and the manager of technical training is a member of the employers group.

As part of the Compact, Ford gives teenagers work experience at its technical training centre in Dagenham. Managers from the company also go into the schools to work with the children and teachers return the visit with a stint at the technical training centre.

The company also sets goals for the pupils at local schools. These are not based on academic achievement, but discipline. (Among other targets youngsters must reach 80% punctuality and 80 per cent attendance.) If they achieve these goals they can become Compact students on a Ford training programme.

Says Baker: 'In this way, Ford hopes to tackle the underlying causes of low educational standards among ethnic minorities.'

Bringing more ethnic minorities and women into the workforce meant that Ford had to train more than 1000 supervisors to deal with any problems that arose such as racial bullying and sexual harassment. Ford issued a booklet in the summer of 1990 advising its supervisors how to deal with discrimination. The company also runs race relations courses. Managers, shop stewards and supervisors attend a two day workshop called 'Race and Equal Opportunities'. Participants are encouraged to plan positive steps to counter discrimination. They study the importance of equal opportunities to the company, how racial prejudice and racial discrimination can arise and the legal aspects of these issues. 'Improving Race Relations at Work' is another workshop, this time aimed at senior managers. It covers much of the same ground but also looks at strategic and policy issues in race relations.

The results of the equal opportunities policy can already be seen at Ford. At the beginning of 1989, 4.9% of the technical training centre intake was female and just four per cent were from ethnic backgrounds. By January 1990 7.9% of trainees were girls and 9.1% were from ethnic minorities.

Says Baker: 'Youngsters from ethnic backgrounds will be able to see people like themselves in skilled posts and will hopefully be more encouraged to apply. It is a long slow process and we don't expect to see results for at least five years.'

Ford has also been concentrating on increasing the number of women and ethnic minorities in graduate jobs. Working in conjunction with sixth form colleges in Tower Hamlets, Redbridge, Newham and the North East London Polytechnic, Ford developed a pre-degree foundation course at the polytechnic for 15 youngsters between 18 and 19 years of age. These students have been assessed by their sixth form teachers as having potential but needing help to get through their A levels. Ford provides a bursary plus tuition fees for these students during the extra study year.

In the first year of the scheme, 13 students were selected and nine actually attended the course. All nine went on to take up places on engineering, management or manufacturing courses at North East London Polytechnic in September 1989. The other four received grades that were good enough to reach university on their own, so they were able to join directly a long-standing graduate scheme that sponsors 70 students a year.

Says Baker: 'Our vice president for manufacturing had the idea for a pre-degree course when he was in South Wales. We adapted the idea. East Londoners would be more enthusiastic about a scheme that would send them to a college in their area. It would be harder to recruit for the course if the students then had to go to South Wales to study.'

As part of the drive to encourage more minorities into the workforce, Ford has updated its graduate brochure to include large colour pictures and case studies of minority employees. The aim is to increase the graduate intake from 8% ethnic minorities and 29% women.

Case study: *TSB plc*

The TSB has a four-point equal opportunities strategy, which involves establishing closer links with ethnic community groups in the West Midlands, improving its recruitment literature, providing pre-recruitment training and revamping its recruitment advertising.

The West Midlands initiative started as a 10-company YTS project. The TSB forged links with community groups such as the Handsworth Breakthrough, the Birmingham community organisation, Accafess and the Commission for Racial Equality. Through these initiatives, TSB showed that it was interested in the ethnic community and within a year ethnic minority applicants to the bank rose from 12 to 20 per cent.

The TSB has also run pre-recruitment training courses in London with the South West College, which had a 90% ethnic minority intake. The TSB provided job guarantees to those who successfully completed the course and 16 were appointed in the first year.

One of the lessons the equal opportunities department at the bank learned from the programme was that a lot of well-qualified blacks did not apply to the financial sector, because they feared discrimination. Some of those who applied for the training course were able to be appointed immediately, because they already had the necessary qualifications.

Senior management at TSB stressed that commitment should come straight from the top, if a programme is to be successful. At the TSB, each regional chief executive is responsible for equal opportunities and is accountable to the group chief executive on a quarterly basis. Each regional executive also has to produce an action plan and monitor the composition of the workforce in his or her region.

2.1.2 *The disabled*

According to the Royal Association for Disability and Rehabilitation (RADAR) in April 1988 there were 374,238 disabled people registered with the Department of Employment. But as Mr. Tim Eggar MP for Enfield North stated in April 1990, only 23.3% of private sector employers who are required to have 3% or more disabled workers, actually do so. Only 4.7% of public sector companies fulfilled their obligation.

A spokesman from RADAR points out that 69% of the general population of working age are in employment, but only 31% of disabled people of working age are employed. A recent survey by the Spastics Society also found that two-thirds of employers discriminated against job applicants who admitted they had a disability, even though the disability would not affect their ability to do the job. The society is pressing for anti-discrimination legislation along the same lines as for race or sex.

Among the reasons companies most frequently put forward for not hiring the disabled are:
– trade unions are often more concerned about finding jobs for the able bodied, who they insist must be given priority
– disabled people will have greater absenteeism and add to insurance costs because they are a safety risk
– disabled people can't work as efficiently as the able-bodied.

In practice, most of these assumptions turn out to be at best only partially true. Some years ago, the US chemical company Du Pont conducted a survey of the safety, attendance and job performance records of 1425 disabled employees. The employees had a variety of handicaps, including partial paralysis, lost limbs, deafness, blindness and chronic heart ailments. The disabled people were found to be better on all three counts than the able-bodied people. In job attendance, for example, 79% had a better than average record. In job performance, only 9% were below average while 37% were above average. In terms of safety, they also outscored the able-bodied. More than 50% had a better than average record. As a bonus, the study also recorded how long they had been with the firm. It found that 90% had been there an average or longer than average period. There was comparatively low labour turnover among the disabled.

One of the keys to getting the most out of disabled workers is to treat them as much as possible like everyone else. Disabilities can often be overcome through training or minor adjustment to equipment. Most companies experienced in this area avoid creating enclaves of disabled employees or sheltered workshops. In such an environment, it is inevitable that the employees will adapt to a rule where they are not expected to perform as well as others. Most disabled workers neither ask nor desire to be mollycoddled.

A French bank has an innovative approach to the disabled. It runs its own training school for the handicapped where it teaches them basic banking skills. It started the school in 1965 because so many of its employees had handicapped children who could not find work. As soon as the students reach the proficiency level of regular employees in skills such as book keeping or dealing with bonds, they are transferred to a full-time job in one of the bank's branches.

Companies like General Electric in the US or Cadbury Schweppes in Bourneville, Birmingham, have made it a policy to incorporate ease of access for disabled people in all new offices and factories. Aids that can make access much easier for disabled workers include non-stop flooring handrails on stairways and lower than normal drinking fountains and public telephones. The most practical way to establish where access improvements are needed is to ask handicapped people. It is very hard for the able-bodied to appreciate the difficulties of being confined to a wheelchair or of lack of sight.

The mentally handicapped also have a role to play in today's workforce. All that it requires is that the personnel department thinks a little harder about job content.

Supermarkets and large stores are increasingly using mentally handicapped people to stack their shelves. These workers gain immense job satisfaction from doing dull repetitive tasks and by doing so they free other workers to do more demanding work elsewhere. Fast food outlets are using them to clean the tables and floors throughout the day, leaving others to man the tills.

While there are problems with using mentally handicapped workers – they need more supervision, they cannot be hurried because it destroys their concentration and they may have to be transported to and from work – the benefits tend to outweigh the disadvantages.

Case study: *The Littlewoods Organization*

The Littlewoods Organization, one of the UK's largest private companies, is such a leader in the field of equal opportunities for the disabled that other firms come to it for advice. The company employs over 400 full-time staff who are registered as disabled and 500 staff who are not registered, but have disabilities such as epilepsy and multiple sclerosis. The company, whose business activities include 114 chain stores and a home shopping agency, employs over 36,000 people, of whom 8,500 work in Merseyside. The projects are blessed with strong leadership at boardroom level and well briefed and motivated senior and middle management. The equal opportunities committee is chaired by John Moores, a member of the board of directors. Support for the programme is given on day to day basis by the group chief executive, Desmond Pitcher.

Littlewoods initiated its equal opportunities policy in 1967. A general review of the previously race-based equal opportunities programme in the mid-eighties resulted in the publication of a code of practice, which recognised the need to broaden the policy to include gender and disability.

The code was completed in 1985 and was fully launched in 1986 with a booklet, which was sent to all managers, and a leaflet, which was sent to all members of staff. The code covers recruitment, recruitment publicity, selection process, training, career development, job satisfaction, terms and conditions of employment, part time employment, responsibility of management supervisors, ethnic minorities and religious beliefs, employees with domestic responsibilities, equal opportunity appeals procedure.

Among the initiatives Littlewoods has undertaken is to provide ramp access to its buildings, special toilets and other adaptations such as visual fire alarms in buildings where the deaf work. Management has also changed the job content to help the disabled do as much as possible.

A number of disabled pupils from the School of the Good Shepherd, Litherland, Merseyside have undertaken work experience at the Littlewoods site in Crosby. The visit was so successful that one of the children was offered a place on a company YTS scheme.

Thanks to its comprehensive programme for the disabled, the company was presented with a Manpower Services Commission's Fit For Work award in 1981 and again in 1985.

Checklist
1. Have you set yourself targets to employ a certain proportion of disabled people by a set date?
2. Have you checked access to factory and office buildings? Can disabled people get into your premises to work?
3. Look at the work stations and the duties of the job. Think of ways of making the tasks disabled-friendly. Install a screen reader so blind people can work on your computers and word processors.
4. Can some work be put out to disabled home workers?
5. Are there any tasks that can be profitably done by mentally handicapped people?

2.1.3 *Working for women*

According to the Henley Centre for Forecasting, women are expected to make up more than half of Britain's workforce by the turn of the century. At present they occupy one in three jobs. Henley expects three quarters of all new jobs to be filled by women and the proportion of women in full time professional occupations or senior management will increase from its present 5%.

Leading corporations, such as the High Street banks, are trying to make it easier for women to return to work after having children, and to encourage older women to work. For example, Lloyds offers career breaks to both men and women who have been with the company more than five years. Its ultimate aim is to encourage all eligible staff to take a career break. The bank will give consideration to requests for several breaks with a total absence of not more than five years and guarantees that the employee comes in at the stage he or she left. This is mainly because of a predicted skills shortage. Nonetheless the lead has generally been taken by more progressive and enlightened employers.

The range of measures such companies have taken to encourage more women back into the workplace, and into management positions, is considerable. Among them:

Company sponsored childcare
Midland Bank was one of the first organizations to tackle the issue when it opened a 46 place nursery in Sheffield in October 1989. The nursery, which charges £35 for each child, is subsidized by the bank and is the first of 300 that it plans to open within the next four years. The children, from six months to five years,

will be supervised by seven staff from Kids Unlimited, who run employee creches. Midland's equal opportunities director, says: 'When a woman gives up a job to have children, employers lose immeasurable training and experience.'

First Leisure employs women of all ages in its bowling centres and has solved the child care problem in a slightly different way. Each centre has a children's playroom which operates during the day for customers who bring in their under-six-year-olds. Staff also take advantage of the supervision by qualified child minders.

Positive recruitment and career development

B&Q, the DIY chain, is making special concessions to bring women into its workforce by offering part-time junior managerial posts and through an advertising campaign aimed at women.

B&Q explains: 'Female managers often don't apply to work with us because DIY is perceived as a male orientated business. In the light of demographic change, we need to attract more women. This can only be a positive move for us, since our surveys have shown that women stay longer with the company. Their appraisal ratings are very good, too. They are more consultative and see the person as a whole when it comes to people management.'

Part of B&Q's campaign includes promoting women into positions which have previously only been held by men. The aim is to give a strong signal to the business that the company is serious about having women in senior management positions.

At store level, the company introduced in late 1989 a flexible scheme designed to bring more mums back to work. About a dozen women in the South East have been employed during school term times, leaving them free to look after their children in the holidays. The posts are filled by students during vacation periods. B&Q says: 'We introduced the scheme in the South East, where we currently have major recruitment problems, and so far it has been very successful.'

Case study: The Littlewoods Organisation

In recent years, Littlewoods has changed selection and recruitment policies, introduced training in good practice and set targets for the promotion of women in the company. The result is an increased percentage of women at all levels of management. The company recognises the organisational and personal barriers which prevent women rising to senior management positions. It is considering a number of special initiatives such as child care provision, improved maternity leave, job sharing and part time employment. Littlewoods also operates a career break scheme designed to encourage more employees to return to work. These people are sent regular information packs, including briefings, current vacancies and news. Managers are nominated to look after staff on career breaks. Career breakers are also invited to departmental meetings and have access to a support network arranged by the personnel department. They are also offered part-time work and access to training programmes.

From 1989, the company agreed to reduce the qualifying period for maternity leave from two years to one, to double paternity leave to 10 days and to provide equivalent benefits to staff adopting children as well as time off with pay for relevant court hearings. Other initiatives taken by the company include education, training of women in the workforce and encouragement to young women still in education through educational materials, company information sessions and work experience schemes. In 1987 Littlewoods was presented with the Woman in Management award.

Career break management

Norwich Union was concerned at the loss of the training investment it had made in women who did not return after maternity leave. It recognised that some mothers prefer a career break instead of returning to work after the statutory 29 weeks maternity leave after confinement. For this reason, the insurance company has introduced a career break scheme, under which staff with at least two years service can take a break of up to five years following maternity leave.

Norwich Union offers the career break scheme at management's discretion, rather than as a right for all employees and there will be no guarantee of re-employment. However, for those who are chosen there will be up to two weeks paid work each year to update on procedures and undertake further training. Other steps will be taken to maintain regular contact. The women will return to the same grades they left. After a trial period, each will be reappointed as a permanent staff member and will be credited with full back service in respect of her pension arrangements.

Norwich Union also revamped its maternity leave in mid 1989. Under the new arrangements, when an employee returns from maternity leave, her period of absence will now count as pensionable service as soon as she continues to work for the Norwich Union for a minimum of a further six months. If an employee should die during her maternity leave, a lump sum payment of three times her salary will be made to her estate in the same way as if she had still been working. Maternity leavers still benefit from insurance premium discounts and can still continue as staff agents during their time out.

Once the woman has returned to her former post the company will pay for any additional mortgage costs incurred through the loss of mortgage allowance during maternity leave.

Many women are capable of coming back into full time employment after their children have grown up, but are worried about being able to cope with the pressures after spending several years at home.

Returners Limited, Hatfield Heath was formed in 1989 to deal with the problem. It runs programmes to encourage women to return to work for a consortium of companies including Thorn EMI, Tesco, B&Q and Network South East. The scheme, which started in late 1989, consists of four weeks confidence building with training in aspects such as assertion and interviewing. The women then go for six weeks work experience with one of the consortium companies. Returners Limited reports that the scheme has been highly successful and that most of the women are taken on after their work experience period.

Flexible working times
Flexible working hours are now common in many service industries and a few manufacturers. For example, women at the head office of a large building society can work evenings, leaving them free to look after the children during the day. Retail stores already offer a form of flexible hours where women can choose the hours to fit around the children's school times. Many other companies are breaking the old nine to five monopoly and taking a closer look at leaving the office open until 9pm and at weekends. Annual hours, or flexible working years, are also slowly growing in popularity.

Job sharing
The champion of job sharing in the UK is New Ways to Work, a London based organization funded by the London Borough's Grants Scheme. One aspect of its work is to help companies design and implement job sharing as a flexible working option.

Job sharing involves two or more people sharing one or more full time jobs between them. They share the work and the pay, the holidays and benefits. It is now an accepted way of easily introducing part time hours into areas of traditional full time work. Job sharers may work mornings or afternoons, two to five days a week or three shorter days. The type of work determines how it is shared out. The sharers divide between them the status and promotion prospects of traditional full time staff. Job sharing does not require changes in establishment arrangements or employment structure.

For example, secretary Deborah Wilks is 24 years old and before having a baby boy she was a medical secretary with an international company in High Wycombe, Buckinghamshire. A major computer shopping company was able to offer her a job share with another woman who was looking for part-time work. Deborah is able to earn more as a secretary than as a shop assistant, which was the only other post open to her because of the hours she could work. And during the school holidays, her job share stays at home to look after her child while Deborah can pick up the extra hours.

She explains; 'I was fully trained as a word processor operator and medical secretary, so I do most of the typing. My colleague does filing, phone queries and basic typing. But the job share means that she now has the chance to learn more secretarial skills and I can keep up to date with modern office procedure. When my little boy goes to school, I will be able to apply for higher calibre jobs with confidence or go further with this company.'

She adds: 'The job share has been a great success and I feel very lucky to get the chance to do it.'

Case study: *The Boots Company*

The Boots Company has 38 job sharers within its retail division, 38 on its register and a husband and wife among others are in the pipeline. The jobs include pharmacists, sales managers and senior sales assistants. The scheme, launched in 1988, allows job sharing at senior assistant and supervisor levels and above in the non-pharmacy grades and at pharmacy manager level and above.

The scheme was discussed with area managers before it was fully developed. Fears initially expressed by line managers were found to be groundless. Now area managers are behind the scheme and there have been no negative comments from line managers.

Boots feels that the additional costs of employing job sharers are minimal, particularly when compared with total payroll and the cost of replacing lost staff. As the company already has many part-time staff as well as people working term time and variable hour contracts, administration is not a problem. However, it concludes that the training costs may well be higher since job sharers require individual training. In some stores, sharers work three days each to cover a six day opening; in others they work mornings or afternoons or combinations of days and half days. The suitability of each particular job for sharing is considered individually and so far there have been no unsuitable cases. Boots believes that because job sharers work at times which suit their own commitments, they give 100% effort. By reducing turnover, the company can make savings on recruitment costs and on the training of new pharmacy managers. Boots feels there will be a slow build up in numbers of job sharers and is now looking forward to job sharing in store management.

Homeworking

Another increasingly popular option taken by forward thinking companies to help women retain their skills during child-rearing is allowing them to work at home. Dorothy Davies, systems development manager at British Telecom, uses home working as a way of keeping a highly trained workforce. Davies now has some of her most valued programmers and analysts working Telecom computers in spare rooms from Wimbledon to mid Wales. The programmers' computers are fed their work through modems during the night at cheap rate.

ICL has taken to home working so enthusiastically that it even has home based managers, because it found that on site managers did not know how to manage a home based workforce.

Assertiveness training

Assertiveness training is an increasingly popular way of helping women realise their own potential and overcome hesitancy to promote themselves. Among companies that run such courses is Ford. Its courses, run in worktime since December 1988, are targeted at middle graded women, such as accounts assistants, who might not reach their potential without help. They aim to identify the skills, qualities and abilities that the participants already have and examine how these can be developed further; and to help participants improve their abilities at listening, assertiveness, negotiating, coaching and decision making.

Rank Xerox, ICI and Southern Electricity are tackling the same problem. They have installed an open learning course 'Moving into Management' designed to help women build their own career plan, behave more confidently and develop an individual management style. The course has been put together with financial assitance from the Local Government National Training Board and the Co-operative Bank.

It isn't just companies which need to look closely at equal

opportunities for women. Business in the Community (BiC) recently published guidelines for Training and Education Councils, stressing the role that TECs have in demonstrating and encouraging good practice. BiC suggests that TECs should:
– break down traditional assumptions and prejudices about who does what at work by influencing trainers and employers
– take women fully into account in their assessment of the labour market
– address work and family issues by stimulating family support, particularly through collaborative childcare options and flexible working practices
– encourage training and enterprise service providers to improve access for women
– stimulate employers to invest in women's training and employment and to develop the skills of women already at work
– examine their own position on equal opportunities and the role of women in the workforce as well as those of their providers and staff. It is not enough for equal opportunities just to be included in a mission statement or general policy.

Checklist
• Do you have a coherent, written policy and plan for the recruitment and promotion of women?
• Do you employ a wide spectrum of mechanisms to overcome the problems of women's employments? – e.g.

- childcare provision
- positive recruitment and promotion activities aimed at women
- career break management
- flexible working times
- homeworking
- assertiveness training

• Do you monitor the proportions of women at each level of management?
• What proportions of senior and middle management are female now?

2.1.4 *Religious discrimination*

For most of the UK, religious discrimination is not regarded as a significant problem. For Northern Ireland, however, it is the most critical employment issue after unemployment itself. Our case study examines how Shorts has tackled this highly sensitive issue.

Companies in the rest of Britain should be sensitive, however, to the special circumstances of Muslim employees from Asia and Africa. Special dietary and religious observance requirements need not be troublesome to implement if the reasons are understood and they are planned well in advance. Some companies – for example, some airlines – have also recognised that there are benefits in putting this experience to use in improving service to customers.

Case study: *Shorts*

Shorts, Northern Ireland's biggest private employer, has conducted an affirmative action programme to try and boost the number of Catholics in its work force and is held up as an example of good employment practice by the Northern Ireland Office.

The affirmative action programme started in 1983 after a survey in the engineering industry found that Catholics were discriminated against for skilled jobs. Between 3% and 8% of Shorts' skilled workers were Catholic against 26% of the population as a whole in Greater Belfast. Only 6% of apprentice recruits were coming from Catholic schools.

The company recognised it had to employ more Catholics. The programme included advertising in Catholic newspapers, increasing contacts with Catholic schools and greater flexibility in the requirements for entry into the company's technician apprentice scheme.

The number of Catholics employed is now about 12% of the 7,700 work force. The mid term target is 25% of recruits being Catholics (i.e. virtual equality of representation).

John Freeman, a former Shorts shop steward and regional secretary for the TGWU transport union, says: 'The shop floor used to come under a tremendous amount of pressure from hardliners. While I don't doubt that there is still a certain amount of that feeling about the place, it bears no relationship to the atmosphere that existed before.'

2.1.5 Age discrimination

When unemployment reached its peak in the early 1980s, people over 45 were among those who felt the effects most strongly. Many newspaper articles focused on the waste of talent as well-qualified unemployed people found themselves 'too old' for many employers. The UK does not have age discrimination legislation, as do many parts of the United States. But the socially responsible company will want to ensure that this group, too, receives fair treatment in employment.

Companies that do operate age discrimination are losing a valuable resource. A study by US assurance company Bankers Life and Casualty compared the absenteeism rates of 128 randomly selected employees under 65 and 128 over 65. Bankers Life has a long standing policy of encouraging older workers and has little hesitation about hiring people over the normal retiring age of 65. The study showed that only 13 of the under 65s had a perfect attendance record compared with 34 of the over 65s. The under 65s had on average, twice as many half day absences as the over 65s. When employees over 65 became incapable of doing their job, the company found that they usually retire themselves without the need for hints from above.

B&Q opened a store in May 1989, which was staffed completely by the over 50s within six months. B&Q explains: 'Over 7000 people responded to our national campaign. We opened the store for two reasons. Firstly because the demographic changes forced us to look at our recruitment policies and secondly, we wanted to make a statement that we were interested in taking the older person seriously.'

Supermarket chain Tesco has also reaped enormous rewards from its campaign to recruit older people to work in its stores. The number of over 55s employed by the retail group had risen from about 2,000 to almost 5,000 by the end of 1989.

Its campaign 'Life Begins at 55' not only attracted people in the target age group, but also brought in a large response from people in their 30s and 40s and, unexpectedly, from people who were past retirement age.

Following the campaign, the company now permits employment up to the age of 70 and has equalized its normal retirement age at 65, although an existing employee can be re-engaged at that age and provided with continuous service into the future, subject to an annual health check.

Pat Lennon, retail personnel director at Tesco, identified three specific advantages to be gained from employing mature people. Firstly, older people had been customers themselves for so long that they scarcely needed any customer service training. Secondly, they rarely took time off because they had been brought up at an earlier time when working values were different and people did not have days off for minor illnesses. Finally, younger employees felt more comfortable going to an aunt or uncle figure for advice rather than consult a supervisor of similar age. This has had a positive impact on the turnover of younger employees.

Checklist
1. Make it clear on publicity material that job vacancies are open to people of all ages.
2. Check hiring practices. Do you ask applicants for a photograph of themselves?
3. Base selection criteria on the real physical needs of the work rather than on simple age criteria.
4. Monitor the age distribution in the company and if possible compare that to the composition of the local working community.
5. Improve and expand appraisal systems so that older workers know how they are performing.
6. Examine closely corporate policies on retirement. Can workers be allowed to work beyond 65?
7. Do you have difficulty getting staff? Have you thought of positive discrimination towards the older worker?

2.1.6 Broader issues of discrimination

Some forms of discrimination appear to make business sense when viewed narrowly. For example, most companies will reject job applicants with criminal records. Indeed some companies go to considerable lengths to weed out anyone with 'criminal tendencies'. Similarly, people who have been unemployed for a long period because they have obsolete or inadequate skills are difficult to hire because they frequently take a long time to become productive.

However, opportunities to help both these disadvantaged groups do exist. Employers can now arrange fidelity bonds, underwritten at Lloyds. Apex fidelity bonds indemnify the company against any losses attributable to dishonest behaviour by the ex-offender, as long as the offence is not related to the job opening in question (e.g. it would not cover putting someone previously convicted of embezzlement in charge of the company accounts).

A number of companies are also participating in a Business in the Community initiative to help long-term unemployed. Through what it calls "Customised Training", companies put unemployed people through a tailor-made training programme, which leads to a guaranteed job interview, or a guaranteed job. Pilot schemes for this approach since 1987 have been highly successful. For example, William Hill/Mecca Bookmakers have employed 11 trainee managers using the scheme and Debenhams in Northern Ireland employed 67 sales assistants. Other companies which have been involved in pilots include Barclays, British Telecom, Express Dairies, John Laing, Lloyds Bank, McDonald's Restaurants, J. Sainsbury, TSB and the International Stock Exchange.

2.2 Developing talent

Companies which do not provide opportunities for employees to develop their talents almost invariably experience high labour turnover and problems of motivation. The commercial arguments for continuous improvement of everyone in an organization are well-rehearsed. Yet the UK is near the bottom of the European league in expenditure on training and development.

It is no coincidence that companies which take their social responsibilities towards the external community seriously, also put significant resources into growing their employees' skills and abilities. Many of these companies now include training as a major plank of their business strategy.

One convenient way of classifying employee development is as follows:

- basic employment skills
- skills training
- management development

2.2.1 *Basic employment skills*

In spite of free and compulsory education the UK still has a substantial section of the population who cannot read and write. Many others suffer problems of innumeracy. Many companies have hidden literacy and innumeracy problems. A whole generation of workers had their studies disrupted during the Second World War; others missed school because of ill health. Still more had to stay at home to look after sick relatives or brothers and sisters. And a significant proportion of workers can only read and write their own language fluently and are handicapped in English.

Often their needs are invisible. They have developed complex survival skills such as buying newspapers they cannot read. They rely on their families to fill in forms. When they are unable to carry out instructions, they go sick or find ways of avoiding the issue. They and often their companies often regard their illiteracy as a personal inadequacy.

Ford is one company that has set about rectifying the problem and for a number of years has used the Industrial Language

Training Association to run English language courses for those of its employees, mainly hourly paid, who want it.

Checklist
- Are you aware how many employees in your company have a literacy/numeracy problem?
- Do you have a specific remedial programme?

2.2.2 *Skills training*

The government wants the entire British workforce to be taking part in training schemes by 1992, according to targets set by employment secretary, Norman Fowler. Speaking at a Business in the Cities conference in December 1989 he demanded that by 1995 all companies should report to shareholders and investors on their training activities and that by 1992 there should be a comprehensive and effective framework of effective training organizations. The aim, he maintained, was for Britain to become a high productivity, high skill economy, leaving labour intensive unskilled work to developing nations.

However, a survey of Scottish companies carried out last summer by Strathclyde University showed that over a quarter of companies did not provide a single day's training for their managers and supervisors. The survey also highlighted the difference in training approach between large and small companies. More than 42% of small firms failed to put any money into management training compared to 15% of medium sized companies and 5% of large companies.

A recent CBI Vocational and Education and Training Task Force calls for a new assault on Britain's poor training record and demands that employers are awarded with an 'Investors in Training' tag if they follow 10 key characteristics of a good training employer.

These are:
1. The ability to create a 'vision' of the future, relating the business to its people and emphasising their role.
2. The adoption of a business plan covering future skills needs.
3. Identifying training objectives and plans.
4. Setting training targets to raise employees skills and qualifications by certain dates.
5. Allocation of resources to training as a priority and setting of training budgets to include the wage costs of training.
6. Agreement on a common definition of a training activity,

reporting on it to managers, employees, investors and share-holders and assigning responsibility for training within the organisation.

7. Support for self development and providing the employees with opportunities to pursue relevant qualifications, a regularly revised action plan as part of a careership profile and access to independent careers guidance.

8. Establishing a training structure through training audits, skills assessment, action plans and guidance, coaching and monitoring.

9. Evaluation of expenditure.

10. Focus on external training initiatives such as the Local Employer Networks, industry training organisations and the Management Charter Initiative.

Case study: *International Computers plc*

International Computers (ICL), a major operating company within the STC Group, employs 22,000 people in 70 countries. It has started an 'Investing in People' programme, which is designed to increase training and development for all of them. A handbook, used by all ICL managers and their staff to define each individual's development needs, covers objective setting, appraisal, performance improvement, career development and training. Each employee regularly discusses his progress with his manager to ensure that he is maximizing his potential. At the discussion, they define the objectives each employee should achieve in order to contribute fully to the company's business and appraise the employee's contribution, while looking at ways to improve it. They also determine the most suitable career direction for each employee and the specific action plans needed to achieve this. Finally they plan the necessary training within a company training budget of £25 million a year. Through such programmes, ICL aims to achieve the fastest possible growth for both individuals within it and for the company itself.

Case study: *Rover Group*

Vehicle manufacturer The Rover Group launched 'Rover Learning Business' in mid 1990 to help its 40,000 people develop their talents. The scheme has a training budget of about £30 million a year and will operate in partnership with academic institutions including Warwick University, City University and Leeds Polytechnic, which will help provide some of the courses.

Its main product is the design and development of training courses and materials in response to the demands of Rover employees. The training departments of each Rover plant will act as 'franchisees' to 'Rover Learning Business'.

Some companies have recognised the value of having employees develop skills not directly related to their current work. For example, Ford and the trade unions representing the company's 44,000 hourly paid and salaried employees are running an Employee Development Assistance Programme, which offers employees a wide range of educational courses as well as schemes to encourage a healthier life style.

Case study: *Ford Motor Co.*

Ford's Employee Development Assistance Programme, which is funded by £1.8 million a year from Ford and £150,000 from the government, is believed to be the first of its kind in British industry.

Everyone from factory line workers to management is eligible to apply for up to £200 a year for approved training and assistance. Under the scheme secretaries will be funded to do accountancy training, but accounts assistants will not be funded for accountancy courses since that is covered by other company schemes. The fund does not give money for hobbies or recreational activities.

Set up after the 1987 contract negotiations, the programme is administered jointly by the unions and the management at national and plant level. The Local Joint Programme Committees will approve applications for grants, provide necessary services and identify suitable courses to meet local needs.

Ford is offering financial support for employees who want to do basic academic courses, higher educational and Open University qualifications or vocational and careers skills. Employees have enrolled for courses from bricklaying to weight watchers, with languages the most popular choice. Says a company spokesman: 'We thought only 5% would apply in 1989, which was the first year, but 13% came forward and the number has been rising all the time.'

He adds: 'It is a very positive programme because it demonstrates unions working together with management for the good of the workforce. Employees are getting the chance to exercise their minds which makes them brighter and more alert.'

Local Education Assistants, paid for by the EDAP fund, assist employees to find the right course for them and administer the plant's budget.

Jack Adams, a national officer of the Transport and General Workers Union and acting chairman of the trade union side of the Ford National Negotiating Committee, welcomed the scheme saying: 'The joint running of the programme, with trade union representatives having a majority on the committees at national and local level, will ensure that course provision and funding is tailored to meet our membership's needs and that the barriers to access to education and training are removed as far as possible.'

Coca Cola and Schweppes Beverages has a different scheme. Everyone in its main locations has access to Lifetime Learning Links Centres. These are unmanned, but contain learning materials including books, audio tapes, video cassettes covering subjects as diverse as French and financial accounting through to DIY and distribution management. Some centres also have interactive videos and computers available. The centres are open during the day and employees can either drop in and use the resource on site or borrow specific items for study at home.

On sites without a Link Centre people can order learning materials from a catalogue which is updated regularly. CCSB set up the centres because it believes that learning is a lifetime experience and is often more effective when the employee manages it him or herself.

Checklist
1. Does every employee have at least some skills training every year?
2. Do you have a scheme to fund employee self-development?
3. Is continuous learning an element of the corporate mission?
4. Is helping others learn and grow a written part of every manager's responsibilities?

2.2.3 *Management development*

A plethora of reports and studies in the late 1980s identified that the UK lay well behind its international competitors in the attention it gave to management training. One study, by Bath University, revealed that 20% of large companies (those with 1,000 or more employees) provided no formal training courses for their managers at all.

This, it may be argued, is a business rather than a social responsibility issue. But it can equally be argued that companies have an obligation to help managerial employees increase their value to the community. Moreover, the implementation of many of the social responsibility objectives elsewhere in this book is only possible when managers are competent, confident and motivated.

In July 1987, a group of companies, educators and organizations representing business and managers came together with

government to form the Council for Management Education. The Management Charter Initiative now has several hundred corporate members and aims to persuade thousands more to both understand their responsibilities for developing managers and to introduce effective programmes to promote management development. An early element of the MCI's activities was a draft code of practice, the nub of which we reproduce here in lieu of a checklist:
- to improve leadership and skills
- to encourage continuous development
- to provide a coherent framework for self-development
- to ensure management development integrates with work
- to provide access to training
- to encourage relevant qualifications
- to participate in MCI networks
- to strengthen links with management development providers
- to link with educational establishments (to promote management as a desirable career)
- to monitor progress.

2.3 Health, safety and welfare

Companies that take a proactive approach to employee health, safety and welfare benefit in a number of ways.

First and most obviously, they are much less likely to fall foul of the law if employees are injured – costly not only in cash terms, but in management time, bad publicity and, in a growing number of countries, the possibility of imprisonment for executives, who hold the responsibility for ensuring that health and safety legislation is complied with.

Other, less obvious benefits include:
- reduced absenteeism : a high proportion of absenteeism results from occupationally induced ailments. Teaching employees how to avoid these ailments often has a knock-on effect in their behaviour outside work. The net result: fewer days off sick and the potential savings could be huge.
- reduced claims for occupationally induced illness. A number of employers who refused to take any notice of the potential danger from repetitive strain injury (a condition affecting people who use word processor keyboards for long, unbroken periods) now face heavy claims for compensation. At one stage in the early 1980s, well over a quarter of Harland and Wolff's employees were reported to be suing the company for loss of hearing as a result of their work.

- health care premiums: the more employees who need treatment, the greater the expense of company-sponsored health insurance schemes.
- more productive employees: people who are under excessive stress – whether work or domestically induced – cannot give their best to their job. The more rapidly the company can help ease that stress, the faster the employee can return to normal productivity. In practice, some companies claim that people who have been helped through a difficult patch by their employer are more loyal and more motivated to work hard to acknowledge the debt of gratitude.

Case study: *Repetitive Strain Injury*

According to the *Financial Times* (27 March 1990) British companies lose 70 million man-days a year to absenteeism caused by musculoskeletal ailments, such as repetitive strain injury (RSI). In 1989, a Midland Bank secretary, Mrs. Pauline Burnard accepted £45,000 as an out-of-court settlement for RSI. In March 1990, three Inland Revenue computer data clerks received £107,500 between them.

In approaching these issues, companies should have the following objectives in mind:
- *making it difficult for accidents and occupationally induced injuries to happen.* That means having effective systems to make sure that only qualificd and suitable people undertake hazardous jobs; providing training against any hazard, both office and shopfloor or external site; ensuring that tools and equipment are safe; and recording and analysing all accidents or ailments that may be relevant, whether or not there is a legal requirement to do so. In each case, there should be clearly defined management responsibilities and systems for measuring compliance.
   The training issue is probably the most neglected here. Companies in very dangerous operations, such as oil drilling or civil engineering, usually have strong training programmes for everyone who works on site. But relatively few companies provide training for, say, office staff in the safe use of guillotines, or require their field sales staff to take advanced driving courses.
- *monitoring where the hazards lie.* Some US companies insist that suppliers of everything, from cooling lubricants to stationery solvents, provide details of composition and likely hazards from their use. At the very least, this provides a good defence if employees do develop illnesses related to the use of these products.

- *providing a resource, where employees can unburden themselves of stress-inducing problems.*

Checklist

1. Does your company have clearly defined responsibilities for health and safety? Who monitors performance?
2. Does your company know where it might be causing or exacerbating occupational ailments and regularly check to ensure that it does not do so?
3. Does it encourage employees to express their concerns about health and safety at work, and take those concerns seriously?
4. Does it have a confidential counselling scheme that employees trust?
5. Does it encourage good safety practice through education, training and incentive schemes?

Case study: *The Post Office*

In recent years, the Post Office's Health and Safety Executive (POHSE) has earned a formidable reputation through a string of imaginative and comprehensive health projects.

The Post Office's occupational health service started in 1854 in the midst of London's last great cholera epidemic. Scrapped with the formation of the National Health Service in 1948, it was reconstituted in 1969, when the Post Office became a corporation. Today the service employs a full time professional staff of 14 doctors and 42 nurses, plus seven part-time medical staff. This team is responsible for more than 200,000 employees.

Its single biggest project in preventative medecine is free cancer screening for all 37,000 women staff at or near their work. A unit built on the back of a 40 ft trailer tours sites offering cervical and breast screening.

Dr Richard Welch, the Post Office's chief medical officer, explains why the £850,000 service is so important: 'Cervical cancer causes the premature death of 2,000 women in the UK each year, with some 4,000 new cases diagnosed per annum. Breast cancer is an even bigger killer, with some 15,000 deaths each year. These figures are tragic, particularly because patients have an excellent chance of a cure, providing problems are detected early enough. Our campaign makes it simple and convenient for women staff to have comprehensive tests'.

POHSE's responsibilities can be broadly split into two areas:
– the more traditional role of occupational health including identifying and advising on potential hazards in the workplace; finding suitable employment for staff with disabilities; advising staff with health problems

either caused by or affecting their work; the medical aspects of recruitment and early retirement; and providing professional guidance on first aid.

– the instigation and promotion of heath education programmes for all staff. These include encouraging staff to adopt a healthier lifestyle, including exercise and sensible diet; advice on alcohol; advice on the prevention of non-occupational injury and disease; provision of voluntary health checks and screening; and, most recently, specialist counselling on stress and stress-related illnesses and stress prevention actvities.

Recent initiatives include:

– a mobile exhibition which toured larger Post Office sites around the UK. It contains advice and information on coronary heart disease and ways on reducing individual risk; the safety aspects of drinking and driving; demonstrations of life resuscitation techniques. The unit also offers health screening and the chance to learn, from computerized health education modules.

– the POHSE Medibus is an extension of the roadshow and offers health promotion, education and screening actvities to smaller offices.

– The Post Office and the Royal Dutch/Shell Group of Companies, together with the department of Community Medicine, Kings College Hospital School of Medicine, are involved in a comprehensive alcohol education and training initiative known as the King's Project in Industry. It has developed a training package, including a video, which is offered to all managers and supervisors through the Post Office management colleges. It has also been sold to 160 outside organizations, which recognise the necessity of helping staff overcome drinking problems.

– The Post Office has distributed leaflets to all staff on how to give up smoking. Health checks for smokers are available on the Medibus and a simple voting system has been declared, which allows staff to declare their office or workplace a 'no-smoking' area.

The Post Office's pilot stress-counselling programme has attracted a lot of interest among larger organisations. A pilot scheme, which was run in Manchester and Leeds, used specially trained professionals to counsel staff who felt depressed, anxious or showed other stress-related symptoms. While only a small number of those counselled blamed work issues for their condition, most recognised that their enjoyment of and ability to do their job had suffered as a result.

Case study: *Employee Advisory Resource*

Counselling services in the form of Employee Assistance Programmes were virtually unknown in Britain in 1981. It was then that Control Data introduced its own confidential counselling and information service for employees and their families called the Employee Advisory Resource or EAR.

It was so successful and attracted so much interest that in 1986 the Uxbridge-based EAR began to provide an independent service to other organisations. Companies which subscribe provide their employees with:
- instant 24 hour access and response
- expert crisis intervention
- short term counselling and assessment
- consultation and support to managers
- referral to specialist services assessed by EAR
- follow up contact to ensure that individuals have received the help they need.

2.3.1 *Employees with dependent relatives who need care*

One in nine of all full time employees and one in six of all part time workers have an elderly or disabled relative to care for, according to the Family Policies Study Centre. Yet, says the centre, British companies have very inadequate terms and conditions of employment when it comes to assisting such employees.

The charity Opportunities for Women paints an even bleaker picture in its report Care to Work (June 1990). From surveys of 1000 people who stay at home to look after dependent relatives and 2000 people in employment it found that:
- 50% of carers would go out to work, if they could find a job with adequate support facilities
- 50% of people in employment cared for children, the elderly, or the disabled
- 69% of all respondents said that carers' difficulties were not sufficiently recognised in the workplace
- discrimination against carers leads to stress, blocks promotion and bars carers from jobs.

Employers in America, however, are introducing programmes to help carers, recognising that the ageing of the population means that more and more employees will be affected.

American help programmes for carers include an extensive assistance programme by the Hartford based Travellers Corporation. This provides lunch time seminars, care giver support groups, flexible hours and unpaid leave of up to four weeks for personal emergencies. Champion International has established a policy that includes the right of six months leave of absence for a family crisis. IBM has set up a nationwide telephone assistance line aimed at helping employees to assist their elderly relatives,

43

no matter how far away they live from each other. Pepsico has drawn up a resource guide and outline for employees with specific problems.

Dependent health care in the USA is essentially private-sector driven and organizations develop practices tailored to their own needs. People who have to care for elderly or sick charges often have symptoms similar to those related to drug or alcohol abuse, such as fatigue, poor concentration, excessive absences and lateness. As well as losing productivity from such employees, companies incur costs from increased use of the telephone, increased demands on company health services and benefits and unanticipated extended lunch hours or days off. A company policy towards the issue makes it possible to control the costs while helping employees to cope with the stress of caring.

Checklist
1. Have you surveyed your workforce to identify the scale of dependent-relative care problems?
2. Do you know how much it costs your company?
3. Do you have a programme to help employees cope with this situation?

2.3.2 *Caring for pensioners*

The day that they retire is a watershed for most employees. Although many companies have generous pension schemes, and some have schemes of phased retirement, even some of these organizations take the view that the retired employee is no longer the responsibility of his or her former employer.

Yet both the company and the retiree can benefit from a continued relationship. For example:
– some companies make use of retired employees to fill in at peak or holiday periods
– some manufacturing companies bring back retirees on a part-time basis as tour guides; others as part-time tutors for basic skills training of new recruits.

Even if these opportunities are impractical, the caring company can at least keep in touch, by sending the company newspaper, by recognising anniversaries and by inviting retirees to celebrations. This effort can partly be repaid through the ambassadorial role of former employees, who still feel good about the company and its products and services; partly through a recognition among current employees that they will not be forgotten immediately they accept their gold watches.

Case study: *Pilkington Group*

Pilkington intends that its retirees will live a full life in retirement. It helps them to keep physically and mentally fit and independent of institutionalized care, but also supports those who do need such care.

The Pilkington welfare programme consists of a range of cash benefits given to ex-employees or their spouses with at least five years service. These are given at Christmas and birthdays and retirement anniversaries. Food parcels are given twice a year and pensioners receive gifts on golden and diamond wedding anniversaries.

A 'keeping in touch' service is provided for all pensioners by the welfare centre. In addition a quarterly magazine and a talk link cassette for the partially sighted are handed out. Care and support are provided to help pensioners who are financially insecure or sick. This help includes assistance to relieve pensioners' carers.

Pilkington's Charitable Trust Fund finances and administers 90% of the programme. Expenditure is funded from income from investments administered by the trust, with the remaining 10% funded by the company. The welfare programme provides care for 20,000 people in the UK, 11,000 of whom live in St. Helens. The company has plans to broaden the services in the UK and to extend the visiting services throughout the world.

Checklist
1. Do you keep in contact with retired employees?
2. Do you have a scheme/policy to help them in case of genuine need?
3. Do you regard them as a resource?

2.4 Managing dissent

Most of the literature about good management practice emphasises the need to create a common vision, to gain commitment to common goals. Yet the evidence from the majority of companies that fail is that visions are insufficiently tested by constructive criticism. The naysayer, the person who puts a different view that challenges the accepted wisdom within an organization, is all too often regarded as disruptive.

The socially responsible company needs to establish a balance between the need for group cohesion and the encouragement of constructive dissent. It needs its employees (and customers) to feel that, if they inform management about what they consider to be an injustice or malpractice, they will be both listened to and thanked for their efforts. The employee who observes the company is paying inadequate attention to safe disposal of its waste, for example, is a valuable resource. By alerting senior management to the problem, he may save the organization severe damage to its reputation. Left without a channel to register his dissent, that employee may become an internal guerilla, a whistleblower, who forces the company to behave in a way he considers proper, by calling in outside agencies, such as regulatory agencies, the Press, or environmental pressure groups.

Experience shows that, in almost every case where an employee feels compelled to take that step, both the organization and the individual suffer. (Often the individual suffers most, because once his or her identity is made public, they become almost unemployable.)

So, what can you do to bring constructive dissent out into the open? Among other things:

- *Create mechanisms for dissenters to obtain a hearing at senior level*

Some companies employ an ombudsman, often attached to the internal auditing function, or reporting directly to the chief executive. In some cases, a non-executive director can be given the role of corporate conscience. Whichever route is preferred, the employees must know of their right to register dissent and must feel they will not be penalized for doing so.

The US equivalent of Britain's Atomic Energy Authority awards an annual prize for the best dissenting paper by staff. The result is that unpopular opinions are not buried, but openly discussed.

- *Convince people you mean it*

Top management must emphasize that it values, respects and protects the dissenting voice.

3 Responsibilities towards suppliers

The importance of social responsibility towards suppliers – and concern for their welfare – is still only an emerging issue for many companies. Yet there are a number of good commercial reasons for top management to take the issue seriously, particularly regarding the organization's relationships with smaller companies. Among those reasons:

• Many multinational corporations are insisting that their suppliers meet strict quality criteria. They are reducing the numbers of suppliers, in favour of closer relationships with fewer companies, who can guarantee the consistent high level of product and service quality they require. Those companies, in turn, have little option but to insist upon similar relationships with their own suppliers, because they, too, cannot afford for their products and services to suffer from poor input.

• even relatively minor components incorporated into a product, if they are unreliable, unsafe or environmentally unsound, can ruin brands, which have taken years to develop

• small businesses are often both suppliers *and customers*

• suppliers tend to give the best service to customers who treat *them* best. The notion that the biggest customer usually receives most attention is a myth. To obtain excellent service from suppliers, companies must demonstrate that they are valued. The only difference between customers and suppliers is that they are at different points on the same chain.

To a large extent suppliers can be seen as an extension of the large company's own business. Hence they may demand much the same attention to efficiency and solvency as a fully-owned operation.

Companies which have already taken these factors into account are already offering some or all of the following:

• practical help and advice to smaller suppliers

• purchasing policies that ensure that small and local companies have a fair share of the business

- monitoring suppliers' social responsibility performance
- payment policies that help small businesses
- closer arrangements with suppliers through partnership agreements.

3.1 Practical help and advice

Most of the companies that have substantial supplier aid schemes find that the expertise they lend results in cost savings for the manufacture of their supplies and that some of these savings are passed back to them .

The range of areas where the big company can use its resources to aid the small supplier are legion. For example, few small companies have the staff and expertise to evaluate diversification plans adequately. To the big company, however, there is much to be said for encouraging its suppliers to diversify. If the big company needs to slow down production temporarily, any supplier with an excesssive dependance on it may either experience financial difficulties (perhaps leading to closure) or have to pass on its increased unit costs. Some large companies deliberately help small suppliers find additional, preferably non-competitive customers.

The purchasing manager of the small supplier company may have neither the time nor the staff back-up to search widely for the cheapest and best supplies for his own company. However, big companies such as Sweden's Alfa Laval, which have a variety of purchasing specialists, can make their expertise available for mutual benefit.

Some companies, including Marks and Spencer, give suppliers advice and guidance on a wide variety of issues from the design of washrooms to personnel policies. The theory behind this intervention, according to former chief executive Lord Sieff in his book *Don't Ask the Price*, is that attention to employee welfare creates a happier workforce, which in turn means that the quality of the goods produced will be closer to M&S' high standards. Every time a disgruntled worker leaves a supplier, the quality of the output will suffer until the new recruit is fully trained into the job.

Similarly, Ford Europe sends a team of up to 12 people in to help small suppliers turn their businesses round when they come close to unprofitability.

Another Swedish business offers suppliers the use of its empty road vehicles to cut their delivery costs.

Case study: *Marks & Spencer*

Retail firm Marks and Spencer gives technical and personnel advice to its suppliers. The technical team advises on the most modern and cost effective production methods, while the personnel management team shows suppliers how to provide benefits that will encourage a stable, contented workforce. It holds training sessions for suppliers on how to run an employee induction scheme, helps plan the layout of factory canteens and toilets and sends every supplier a news sheet of regular advice on topics such as creches, what equipment to have in a medical room and how to interview a departing employee.

Case study: *British Rail*

British Rail actively encourages small suppliers to compete for the substantial number of orders placed every week, where formal tendering is neither justified nor sensible.

To help small companies obtain a share of its business, it publishes a booklet 'Selling to British Rail', which details British Rail procedures and offers advice.

BR has simplified its purchasing procedures for low value orders to dispense with bureaucracy that might deter the smaller supplier. The booklet lists areas where BR needs supplies, for example, in catering, maintenance and materials. The aim of the booklet, it claims, is to provide sufficient information for potential suppliers to introduce their products and services to the procurement section responsible for awarding contracts for the goods being offered.

Checklist
1. Do you make some of your company's professional expertise available to suppliers?
2. Are representatives from your suppliers invited on your management/customer care/quality courses?
3. Have you carried out research to identify how your suppliers regard your organization as a customer?

3.2 Purchasing policy

Companies rely on the prosperity and health of their surrounding community. One way of ensuring this is to help small firms in the area make the most of business opportunities.

Large firms can examine their purchasing policies to make sure that they are giving a fair share of their business to small, local concerns. They can appoint a member of the purchasing department staff to take responsibility for this area. Sources of advice include: local enterprise agencies, chambers of commerce and Better Made in Britain.

Better Made in Britain was formed in 1983 to focus attention on the increasing penetration of goods from overseas into certain sectors such as the retail and car industry. Sir Basil Feldman, chairman of the firm, Clothing Little Neddy, started the ball rolling when he organized an exhibition where retailers put on display the goods they were importing. Potential UK suppliers visited the exhibition to discuss product specifications, price and delivery with senior buyers.

Following the success of the first exhibition, similiar events were organized for the furniture, clothing, footwear, home furnishings, lighting, carpets, textiles and building products and hardware sectors.

These exhibitions have encouraged people to think positively about buying British goods and £500 million of lost business has been recovered by British industry. Better Made in Britian organizes Challenge days for firms with high import bills. Participating companies open their doors for the day and allow potential suppliers to suggest where their products or services might replace imports. Senior buyers also have the chance to see and evaluate product lines under development. A series of four Challenge days enabled retailer, B&Q, to find UK suppliers for some £18 million worth of previously imported goods.

Better Made in Britain also runs the Regain programme. Many UK manufacturers assemble products in the UK but obtain materials and component parts from overseas. Statistics and details of imported components, raw materials and finished products are often not available, so Better Made in Britain audits industry on a localized basis. From the audit, opportunities in the region can be identified and local businesses encouraged to manufacture in the market gaps.

This approach has been used in West Yorkshire, the North East and the West Midlands. In all three regions, Better Made in Britain was able to point to large numbers of imported components that could be made in the domestic market.

Regain auditors then hold seminars, meetings and exhibitions to inform local businesses, which have relevant capability, about the opportunities for import substitution.Regain also hopes to establish a national database to match up buyers and suppliers.

Case study: *Shell*

Shell UK has wooed small local suppliers as part of a general good neighbour programme. For example, some years ago the company was planning to build a large natural gas plant in Scotland. It was only going to employ 150 people and the proposal was not very popular in the area. Shell's solution was to explain to locals through open evenings the spin-off effect for butchers, launderers and other trades. The building contractor was told to take on as many local sub-contractors as possible. The company had to send a team of advisors to deal with the number of enquiries from local businesses. Under normal circumstances, most of the sub-contracting would have gone to larger, better established firms elsewhere in the country.

Case study: *Halfords*

Halfords, the UK's largest retailer of cycles and car accessories, held a Challenge Day in summer 1989. 180 potential suppliers attended and Halfords was shown so many innovative products that it started discussions with over 25 of them.

Case study: *Kirklees Regain*

Kirklees held one of the first Regain audits in the textiles industry and noted £60 million worth of items that could be supplied locally. The Kirklees and Wakefield Chamber of Commerce and Industry has now extended the Regain project to include engineering, furnishing and general manufacturing.

The project is viewed by opinion formers in the area, such as the president of the Chamber of Commerce, as 'a down to earth attempt to ensure that our local firms know exactly where they can source components and raw materials in the vicinity'.

The Chamber of Commerce Regain team has compiled a database using the information gathered in these audits. Companies can now find out details of finished product ranges and product specifications detailing the quality and quantity of goods purchased as well as technical details, price ranges, delivery requirements and future changes in customer buying criteria. With this information, they can compete more effectively against foreign competitors.

Case study: *Marks & Spencer*

Marks & Spencer prides itself on its buy British policy, claiming that 87% of stock in its stores is British made.

Some critics argue that many suppliers have an unhealthy dependence on Marks & Spencer contracts, giving the company undue power over them – particularly in the setting of profit margins. However, textile industry commentators have argued that it was the company's loyalty to British clothing manufacturers when other retailers sourced abroad, which kept many in business during the recession of the early 1980s.

According to the magazine *New Consumer*, the textile division of the Transport Union (TGWU) criticised M&S, claiming that a number of British sourced finished garments were made from foreign sourced cloth. In response, the company met union representatives to discuss alternative UK based sources. The union commended this move, saying it was in stark contrast to the positions of other major UK clothing retailers.

Checklist
1. Does your company have a formal programme to help small business tender to it?
2. Does your company have a policy and/or programme to encourage local buying; or a Buy British policy?

3.3 Monitoring supplier practices

Companies are increasingly having to take into account the social responsibility behaviour of their suppliers. In particular, following increased media and public concern about environmental issues, it now pays to examine whether a supplier operates its manufacturing and sourcing in an environmentally-friendly fashion. For example, furniture companies which operate a 'green' purchasing policy need to know where their hardwood comes from. They need to ensure that timber suppliers in Brazil, Malaysia, Indonesia and the Philippines are operating sustainable yield harvesting and not indiscriminately chopping down vast tracts of forest.

There is no widespread agreement on how to respond to this particular crisis. Some companies now refuse to stock tropical hardwood. However, others are desperately trying to educate people about the complications of an issue often not properly explored in short newspaper articles or televison news pieces. At the same time, these companies are sending senior managers to visit suppliers, to ensure that they are practising reforestation and are operating sustainable logging.

These issues are only part of a green purchasing agenda and some companies are sending auditors to all their suppliers to examine their manufacturing processes in detail. In many cases, these companies pass the information about the environmental impact of these products onto their own customers.

At the same time, these environmentally-conscious buyers can start putting pressue on wayward suppliers to adopt a more responsible attitude to the environment. Shoemakers and retailers Clarks, for example, made in the 1970s a significant contribution to the world reduction in demand for sperm whale oil to treat shoe leather. It instructed its suppliers that it would reject any leather treated in this way and installed monitoring equipment. Most suppliers agreed, removing an important commercial plank of sperm whale hunting.

Another issue causing similar monitoring is animal welfare. Retail companies are putting pressure on their suppliers to ensure that product research practice meets broad guidelines in this area, producing detailed specifications on how suppliers are expected to handle the issue. For example, several retailers now insist that their suppliers do not test make-up and toiletries on animals. Similarly, some retailers' specifications now stipulate the way animals and fish should be caught and killed.

Case study: *James Latham Group*

James Latham publishes up-to-date information about tropical hardwood deforestation in its company newspaper. It also distributes to customers press releases from the Timber Trade Federation, which discuss the issue from a more general viewpoint.

James Latham buys its timbers from reputable mills, in Malaysia and Ghana, which have especially good records in forest management. But it also buys from Brazil after approval from representatives who have visited the suppliers and checked their approach to logging. All the Brazilian mills it uses practise reforestation. The largest of these mills began planting over 19 years ago and has seeded over 1.6 million trees to date. It is currently reforesting 800-1000 hectares annually.

Other companies have taken slightly different approaches. Major DIY chain B&Q has settled for specifying to its timber suppliers that it only wants wood from a sustainable source. And contract furniture makers, Hands of Wycombe, have developed methods of polishing alternative hardwoods such as ash, beech and oak to produce finishes similar to those achieved with the exotic rainforest timbers. In this way, the company also contributes to the national balance of payments by saving expensive imports of rosewoods and other tropical timbers selected for their richness of colour.

Case Study: *J Sainsbury*

Sainsbury has strict guidlelines for suppliers who kill, catch or use animals. It buys all its meats direct from suppliers, who use known and approved abbatoir sources. It inspects all meat against strict specifications, which cover all aspects of animal welfare and production and follows all relevant legislation and the Farm Welfare Council (FAWC) recommendations.

The company also works very closely with its suppliers to ensure these welfare specifications are followed. Its technologists make unannounced visits to suppliers to check procedures.

Sainsbury's tuna is caught with pole and line rather than by trawling, because it does not involve killing unwanted fish.

In addition, Sainsbury's cosmetics and toiletries are not tested on animals. The company produces a detailed specification and checks the supply of ingredients used. It insists that its suppliers establish that no animal tests for cosmetics or toiletry are conducted on Sainsbury's behalf. Human volunteers test the finished product. Sainsbury's is continuing to look for alternatives to testing on animals.

Case study: *Co-operative Retail Service*

The Co-op has brought in David Bellamy Associates to examine the environmental impact of its branded products from raw material purchase through to manufacture, use and disposal.

It asks suppliers a long list of in-depth questions. In the case of paper supplies, the company wants to know what measures are being taken to control emissions and effluent discharge. Other considerations include what waste and by-products are generated during the manufacturing process and, if these are harmful, how they are disposed of, has the finished product been tested on animals in the last five years and what percentage of the finished product biodegrades, to what timescale? is it recyclable and does it use recycled materials? The information will be used to formulate a greener buying agenda.

Checklist

1. Does your company have formal policies to vet purchases on environmental or ethical grounds?
2. Are you aware of the environmental impact of your suppliers' processes? – If so, have you done anything to change them?

3.4 Prompt payment

According to the Forum for Private Business, a leading small company pressure group, cuts in expansion plans by small businesses suffering from high interest rates and the late payment of bills resulted in the loss of 900,000 potential jobs in 1989.

The Times in June 1990 reports on preliminary analyses by Dun and Bradstreet, the business information services group and a survey by the Forum, which shows in the current period of high interest rates, small firms have been squeezed by large firm buyers, who take much longer to pay their bills – in some cases wiping out suppliers' profits.

Small firms have less flexibility in their borrowing arrangements and therefore are more susceptible to cash flow problems. They can help ensure this doesn't happen by appointing an employee with the authority to chase late payments and by making suppliers aware of his existence.

Some companies admit confidentially that they will pay a small firm quickly, if they have an informal agreement, but our research did not uncover any large concern which was prepared to put that in writing.

N.B. Some states in the United States are considering legislation to penalize persistent late payers. They argue that faster payments all round would speed money flow and increase prosperity for large and small companies alike.

Checklist
1. Do you have a policy of prompt payment to help the cash flow of small suppliers?

3.5 Partnership purchasing

'The motor manufacturers, electronics, food and textiles companies have all been moving to partnership and not confrontation and it could develop into one of the most important trends of the 1990s,' says a consultant to Business in the Community's purchasing campaign.

To emphasize the importance of co-operation and support between supplier and customer, BiC even planned to send out a travelling theatre company to present a play that tackled the issue.

BiC explains the importance of partnership purchasing in the Enterprise Agency newspaper 'Enterprise World': 'The Japanese success in world markets was not down to cheap labour. The secret is teamwork. Suppliers and their customers must work together for quality, efficiency and high production standards.'

It adds: 'The Single European Market will bring increased opportunities and competition to UK businesses and partnership agreements will sharpen supply lines as well as help smaller businesses.'

Many multinational companies aim to cut the number of their suppliers by up to 90%. The remaining suppliers are looked upon as partners with the relationship designed to benefit both parties.

UK partnership purchasers include Marks & Spencer (90% UK-sourced), The Crown Suppliers (90%), Shell UK and Esso UK (from 30 to 80% in five years in the offshore industry) and the The Offshore Supplies Office (90%).

Better Made in Britain also points out the advantages of collaboration.

Partnership purchasing can help the supplying business in a number of ways including:
• advance notice of future trends and specifications, including possible changes of design or quality standards
• debriefing on previous performance
• targets for the future, including financial targets
• help in getting the product right, advice on cost reduction and investment programmes
• guaranteed contracts over a set period to enable investment in new plant and innovation
• agreed delivery times to control inventory levels
• agreed quality standards, testing certification and commitment to zero defects.

The purchasing company also benefits from a number of key factors:
• local supply means secure supply – freedom from dock delays, weather, postal or shipping loss
• easier communication – no language problems, quicker meetings, travel time and costs reduced
• no currency fluctuation risks
• 'Just in Time' delivery schedules can be planned – thus reducing stock holding
• joint development teams can be set up to work on cost cutting, innovation, design and quality.

However, setting up a partnership purchasing system involves a lot of planning at all levels. Senior management, who want to set up a partnership agreement, must first ascertain whether the chairman and chief executive are convinced of its benefit. They must ensure that the purchasing department is behind them and willing to listen. They must also allocate resources to setting up reliable reporting and monitoring mechanisms.

Case study: *Rover Group*

The Rover Group has been developing partnerships with its suppliers since the late eighties. Mike Farnworth, supply agent, explains that the company calls it the 'preferred supplier philosophy'. Previously Rover designed components and developed specifications. It then asked suppliers and contractors to tender for the manufacture of bought out components or the provision of capital equipment and services to Rover plants. Says Farnworth, 'We believe they are the experts in the market place, so they can give us the state of the art in their field.'

Farnworth is responsible for the Purchased Services area of the Facilities and General Supplies Purchasing area at Longbridge, near Birmingham. He said: 'To take plant cleaning as an example, now we ask our cleaning contractors to survey the site for us and develop their specification of work. This is then 'bought off' as the Rover specification by Rover Facilities Engineers and is put out to tender.'

Close co-operation, both in the facilities and the components areas, has led to many advantages for the company:
- shorter lead times to develop components
- improvement in quality
- mutual collaboration to reduce the production costs
- Best Practice teams go out to suppliers and offer help and advice to supply firms. Rover advisers have advised suppliers why certain processes are inefficient and looked to improve labour manning standards, and machine effieciency rates, reduce internal scrap, indirect manning, reject material shipped to Rover and inventory.

Rover's suppliers also gain from the new closer relationship. They receive continuity of business and longer contracts, which have become more competitive. They have also become more competitive and have often won additional contracts elsewhere, on the strength of their close association with Rover.

In principle, Rover will invest in new machinery for its suppliers if it will be more cost effective. But it also expects its suppliers to do the same. For example, a catering company has agreed to share the cost of a new restaurant, retail section and kitchen facilities at Rover.

The company runs a Sterling award scheme for 40 suppliers yearly. To achieve this award, suppliers must meet a set of criteria that includes environmental excellence and quality.

Throughout the twelve months prior to the award, Rover assesses the performance of its suppliers in terms of quality, supply, efficiency, innovation and support to Rover's design, product and manufacturing activities.

Rover's purchasing department issues a statement outlining its mission, values and guidelines giving clear indicators of expected standards.

It is unambiguous in its attitude to suppliers. It states:

'Suppliers have a choice, our ability to purchase the best goods and services depends on their ability to supply. They need to have confidence in our commitment to them to order to invest in the sort of future products that we will need, to the benefit of both parties. We each depend on the co-operation of the other.'

4 Responsibilities towards shareholders

Traditionally, the manner in which companies behave towards their shareholders has depended on three influences – the law, which prescribes the responsibilities of directors and companies; the Stock Exchange, whose rules are aimed at protecting shareholders from various kinds of undesirable exploitation, and accepted practice. All have evolved in the past decade, providing for the most part, greater protection, particularly for small shareholders.

One strong reason for these changes is that well-publicized cases of malpractice have raised public demand for protection. Another is that both the Stock Exchange and the Government have been keen to expand the number of people who own shares. The major privatizations such as British Airports Authority or British Gas have almost all sought to encourage small savers to become small shareholders.

Having a high proportion of small shareholders is expensive – in the sense that they all need to be sent the annual report – but very valuable to top management from the point of view of defence against unwelcome takeover bids. Small shareholders tend, in most cases, to be much more loyal than institutional investors. Nonetheless, the reality for most quoted companies is that the majority of shares will be held by institutions. The way in which the company treats these investors can have a significant effect both on immediate share prices and on how likely they are to give the management team support when it needs it.

Recent research into the attitudes of managers of failed companies indicates that a poor attitude towards investors – failure to keep them informed, to recognize their needs, particularly for information – is often a strong contributory cause of collapse.

Moreover, institutional shareholders, in particular, are beginning to flex their muscles, with the Institutional Investors' Committee demanding much greater accountability from companies' executives. Observes Garry Wilson, a consultant in investor relations for Georgeson International: 'The growing concentration of funds in a relatively small number of institutional investors' hands and the willingness of these investors to voice concern over a company activities has been a strong stimulation to the development of the investor relations industry in the UK.'

For all these reasons, it pays for companies to ensure that they maintain a close and responsible relationship with their shareholders, both large and small.

So, what do shareholders need from the board?

● *Performance.*

For the majority of institutional shareholders and many private shareholders, the primary requirement they will have of the company is that it delivers good dividends and that the shares maintain a high market value. These objectives are backed up by a legal requirement that the company should act in the best interests of its shareholders.

The difficulty arises in defining what is, or is not, in the best interests of shareholders. A couple of decades ago, many companies justified not giving to charities because they considered that this was an unauthorized use of shareholders' funds. It has now become accepted that this is a legitimate means of protecting shareholders' interests, for a whole variety of reasons covered elsewhere in this guide. More recently, debate has centred around the various 'poison pill' options, which companies in the United States have developed to protect themselves against unwelcome takeover bids. Many observers consider that these arrangements are not in the shareholders' interest, because they prevent investors from realizing their investment at the higher share price that would normally prevail in a serious bid.

This whole area represents a minefield for directors, particularly in the United States, where increasing numbers of shareholders are suing board members perceived to be acting against their interests.

One protection for executives is for the board to issue a clear statement of how it perceives its responsibility to shareholders and to have that approval at an annual general meeting (AGM). Some companies include references of this kind within their published mission statements.

Most boards appear to have given little if any consideration to these issues. However, rising expectations from shareholders and the general public are likely to force them onto the agenda over the coming decade.

● *Ease of purchase*

Says Wilson: 'Although the treatment of private shareholders often remains limited to providing tea and biscuits at the AGM, many companies have recognized the act of investment for the small shareholder. They have achieved this through lower dealing charges, dividend reinvestment plans and setting up PEP schemes.'

● *Information*

Shareholders need to know accurately and honestly how the company is performing and what its business prospects are. To put across that information they can use a variety of media, including:

1. *The annual report*

A cynical broker remarks that he only reads annual reports for what they don't say. The great majority of annual reports do little more than fulfil the basic legal requirements of presenting the audited figures. These companies miss an excellent opportunity to market themselves to shareholders and to analysts and institutional investors, who can influence share values. Those companies, for whom a significant proportion of individual shareholders are also customers, can also enhance sales turnover, by encouraging people to support their investments when buying.

Almost all annual reports are made up of a statement by the chairman (often followed by one from the chief executive, if different) and a statement of trading figures for the year, signed by an independent auditor and conforming in presentation to rules set by the accounting bodies.

By custom, companies tend either to include a notice of the AGM in the annual report itself, or send it as an accompanying document. By law, notification must be at least 21 days in advance of the date of the meeting. The company has an option of what other information it should include and how it presents it.

The shareholder needs to be able to understand from the annual report:
– what business the company is in
– how it has performed during the past year and how that compares both with previous years and with its competitors
– what its prospects are for the coming year and what the prospects are for the sector as a whole.

Increasingly, too, many shareholders want to know *how* the company does its business, not only in ethical or social responsibility terms, but from the point of innovation, management style and operating philosophy – all issues which can have an impact on performance.

Unfortunately, relatively few annual reports cover all these needs. (We have encountered several where it was not possible to identify, except by inference, what the main business areas were.)

Moreover, they can be extremely difficult to understand. As Barbara Conway pointed out, in 'Investor Power' 1980:

'Try one basic test. Read through the annual report of the company into which you are thinking of putting your hardearned cash, including the chairman's and director's comments. Then ask yourself the following question: "Do I understand what this business does and how it does it?" '

The basic requirement for most shareholders is that the information should be readily understandable. That means well-written text and well-designed illustrations. Another requirement is that the executives' statements are open and honest. A great many chairmen's statements can best be described as 'not dishonest' – they certainly do not give the impression of great openness. How many chairmen, for example, have admitted to making mistakes (rather than ascribing problems to 'unforseen circumstances' or 'poor trading environment')?

It has been argued that the City requires information to be presented in a formal, jargonized fashion. But stockbrokers and analysts do not necessarily support this view. When Thorn-EMI sent analysts its simplified employee annual report, it found that many analysts prefer to have information in normal language. Moreover, the employee reports contained more information on business strategies and how they were being implemented.

The more information the company can give – for example about directors' shareholdings, responsibilities and external involvements; or about social responsibility issues, such as community involvement or equal opportunities – the more the company will be perceived as open and honest. While disclosure of most of this information is entirely voluntary, the company that does not provide this kind of background is effectively missing an opportunity to enhance the relationship of trust it needs with its shareholders.

2. *The AGM*

AGMs vary from discreet events in isolated hotels, attended by the few, to massive events catering for several thousand.

Key responsibilities for companies here should be:
- to ensure that shareholders have an opportunity to attend.

Few companies, if any, deliberately try to limit the number of shareholders attending the AGM. But relatively few go out of their way to make it easier. A few, such as BAA and British Gas, have chosen to hold their AGMs as centrally as possible, for example, at the National Exhibition Centre in Birmingham, rather than in London. Even fewer have adjusted the hours of their AGMs to meet the needs of those whose work or domestic responsibilities prevent them attending events during working hours.

US company Emhart has experimented with video conferencing to allow shareholders in multiple locations to attend its AGMs. A chairperson at each location ensures that shareholders can ask questions even though they are thousands of miles away. For those who cannot attend in person, Emhart produces a video of the highlights of the AGM, mailing a copy to any shareholder who requests it.

- to ensure that shareholders have the opportunity to ask questions and that they receive fair answers.

Rather than hope that there will be mercifully few questions, so that the meeting can keep to its timetable, responsive companies can *encourage* shareholders to submit questions in advance, for the chairman or chief executive to deal with in amalgamated form. An honest, considered answer will usually – though not always – be of more value to the shareholders than one off-the-cuff.

- to ensure shareholders understand the issues on which they are to vote.

Proxy voters, in particular, need a clear, factual explanation of the arguments, the implications for the company and for the value of their shares. It would also be helpful if companies were to provide more information about directors proposed for re-election.

3. *Stock Exchange and press announcements*

Stock Exchange rules require quoted companies to be accurate in the financial information, including forecasts, that they publish. The rules can be very confining. But companies which restrict their efforts to publicizing financial and product information, lose the opportunity to enhance share value by promoting their community activities.

4. *Ad hoc communications*

Some companies have kept in touch with their shareholders through occasional publications on issues of interest. Others have organized meetings, at which analysts and investors – usually institutional shareholders – are invited to meet the chief executive. These occasions often provide an opportunity for the investors to explain what they expect from the company. However, quoted companies have to be careful not to give preferential access to information at sensitive periods – for example, shortly before the announcement of annual results.

But the small shareholder does not usually receive the same attention. Explains Wilson: 'Communications with shareholders *is* being taken seriously, with more companies providing newsletters with the private investor in mind. However, personal contact with senior management remains limited.'

A handful of companies is also looking at the potential to involve shareholders in measuring and monitoring the quality of the service they provide.

Case study: *BET*

The BET Experience is an imaginative scheme to explain the company's activities to its private shareholders.

BET has about 26% private investors. Many of these had invested in companies that BET later bought. Hence as David Kemp, special projects manager, explains, 'They were not natural shareholders, so we had to communicate with them.'

Says Kemp: 'To expect them to come to the AGM was a bit arrogant and anyway there are high flown legalities associated with such events, so we devised a five year plan to take the BET Experience out to the shareholders. The aim was to be fun and informative. We did not want to be seen to be spending a lot, but it had to be unusual to whet people's appetites and encourage them to attend.'

In 1986, BET held the first event in Leeds. The company took over an old tram shed and issued over 5000 invitations in the form of passports. The theme was 'Coming to an airport' and participants had to register details at passport control. This idea was kept throughout the shows since it provided a handy profile of the shareholders. Once their documentation had been checked, shareholders then had to negotiate an exhibition of BET sites, filling in a quiz card about the locations as they went. Once they had answered the questions, another room was revealed, laid out with food and drink, and entertainment was provided.

Kemp says: 'It worked brilliantly. It was blowing a blizzard on a January night and over 500 people turned up.

'The shareholders went away with the idea that they were the most important people in the world as far as we were concerned,' he adds.

Following the success of this first event, the company took different but just as imaginative roadshows to other venues in Britain. The latest was in Birmingham in 1989.

Anyone who has read BET's annual report for 1990 comes away with an indepth understanding of what the company does, its strategies, where it operates, and who the directors and officers are. This is achieved by simple de-jargonized language and the assumption that the reader knows little about the company, so where possible there are explanations.

On the inside cover, it states in large, bold letters what the company does. In his statement the chairman explores in layman's language issues such as

– What are support services?
– What is the future of support services

The chairman also discusses strategy, acquisitions and legal questions.

The report also lists brief biographies of directors and officers and about six colour pages which use drawings and photographs to describe BET's activities worldwide.

When it made an offer for the personnel company, Hestair plc, it produced detailed information documents for its shareholders. The literature explained the strategy behind the offer and gave details about Hestair again in the de-jargonized language of the annual report.

Case study: *Kingfisher*

Kingfisher believes in direct communications with institutional shareholders. Recognizing that most of them don't see the shops too often, it regularly takes coach parties of investors on store visits. Geoffrey Mulcahy, the chairman and chief executive of Kingfisher, explains at a CBI conference on 'Talking to Institutional Shareholders' in March 1988: 'It's an ideal way of exposing shareholders to the business and the management.'

Mulcahy points out that investor relations should be seen as a prime responsibility of the chief executive of a publicly quoted company and certainly of an alpha stock. He added: 'It's not something that should simply be left to the finance or public affairs departments and increasingly it has a global dimension.' With this in mind, Kingfisher takes every opportunity to convey a coherent and consistent message directly to its stakeholders. As part of this philosophy, in 1988, the Group wrote to all shareholders detailing a blueprint for the future. It outlined the plans for the businesses and summarized them with simple headlines. As Mulcahy explains: 'We believe that fund managers need to know where businesses are being driven. And they need to hear it from those behind the wheel, rather than from the back seat.'

In addition, Kingfisher has up to 50 briefings and 20–25 major presentations a year for shareholders. In this way it addresses up to several hundred existing and potential investors who learn what is happening with the business and over what time scale. Mulcahy says: 'You've got to establish key messages and ensure that they are repeated often enough to be taken on board.'

Checklist

1. Does your company have a public statement of its responsibilities towards shareholders?
2. How informative is your annual report? Have you researched what shareholders think?
3. Does your company make a substantial effort to provide shareholders with information beyond legal and Stock Exchange requirements?
4. Is the AGM designed to meet top management's needs, or those of the shareholders?

5 Responsibility in the political arena

There are few minefields for companies as treacherous as politics, if only because there is often – by definition – no consensus on the 'right' approach. To illustrate the point:

• Many companies responded to international calls to disinvest in South Africa. Others took the view, equally passionately, that they had strong responsibilities towards the black employees in their South African subsidiaries.

• Horticultural companies are under attack for 'stealing the genetic property' of Third World countries in the form of seeds and cuttings. Yet the companies believe they cannot create the disease resistant, high yield new crops the Third World so desperately needs without access to these resources.

• Some developing nations are concerned that the dominance of the international agencies over news reporting in itself constitutes a bias towards Western, developed world values. They wish, instead, to confine local reporting to locally controlled agencies. The international news agencies and newspapers in the Western World regard this as censorship. The two views appear irreconcilable.

5.1 Third World issues

It has to be accepted that technical and mangement skills are in short supply in many Third World countries. But to send expatriates to fill the posts only solves the short term problem and runs counter to local ambitions and sensibilities. It makes good business sense for companies to invest in training local people so that they can take on responsibilities, including the most senior posts, as soon as possible. Significantly, European (including British) multinationals have a relatively high level of indigenization at senior level compared, for example, to Japanese companies.

The company will probably want to include some high fliers from the Third World in its general management programme to develop managers with an international outlook and capacity.

But such training has little relevance to the less gifted managers who will have to manage the shopfloor, or the operators who need technical skills. These, too, have to be catered for.

Developing countries often complain that multinationals are far too concerned with how much hard currency they can export. This concern has frequently led to fiscal controls over repatriating funds. This usually leads to a slowdown in inward investment. India, for example, has recognised only recently that many of its problems in modernizing and achieving growth in GNP during the 1980s were self-imposed. A few multinationals, most notably Coca-Cola, quit the Indian market altogether.

The multinational's traditional response to this issue, and the related question of transfer pricing has been that they benefit the local economy by importing advanced technology and skills into the countries where it operates. More recently, some multinationals have taken the view that the best way to prosper in a market is to demonstrate commitment to it. Among the ways they can do so are:

● make a clear policy of spending profits locally. Where a regional economic alignment exists, the company can probably choose where it uses the money within the economic alliance, as long as it convinces the host country that it really does mean to re-invest its profits.

● assisting in the substitution of indigenous materials and products for imports. Although there are limits to how far this can be done before additional costs resulting from loss of manufacturing scale and from smaller markets make the export of end products uncompetitive, as has already happened in parts of South America, the scope for import substitution is enormous. As many less developed countries have hefty long term debts and constantly agonize over their balance of payments problems, anything a multinational can do to reduce imports will help.

● look for opportunities to locate research and development nearer the problem. Many developing and newly industralized countries have underutilized reserves of technical staff. India and Korea, for example, have surplus computer programmers. Some multinational computer companies have benefitted from tapping this resource. Not only do these companies receive a cost benefit, but they are establishing centres of technical excellence, which they can use to grow their businesses within those countries' expanding local markets.

Unilever has for many years had a policy of conducting R&D

for third world products in the countries concerned. It finds that the research is more relevant to customers' problems if pursued by people who understand local needs. It also contributes to the local economy by identifying local materials that can be substituted for scarce or imported ingredients.

Years of lengthy and inconclusive debate in the United Nations over whether multinationals should be subject to an international code of behaviour have been inconclusive. Yet both sides have moved position considerably. On the one hand, the majority of developing nations now recognise the value of MNCs as powerful catalytic forces within local markets – because they generate an infrastructure of local suppliers – and as importers of technical and managerial skills. On the other, the vast majority of multinationals have recognised that abuse of their power – by, for example, involvement in politics or playing governments off against each other – undermines long-term trading stability. Companies, which want to stay in a developing country and grow there, prosper more when they are recognized as good, local corporate citizens.

As a result, many MNCs have voluntarily adopted and published international codes of practice of their own, that reflect the majority of the aims of previous attempts by Third World nations to impose obligatory standards. These companies usually find that their international codes of practice are beneficial in commercial terms, because they impose common standards of behaviour across their operations, making it easier to prevent misdemeanours by independent-minded local chief executives. Nonetheless, one of the biggest criticisms of multinationals is that they sometimes apply different, lower standards to the Third World than to the developed world.

Cases occur commonly in the areas of:

● *product safety* – e.g. continued distribution in Third World countries of pharmaceutical products banned for safety reasons in the developed world; failure to provide health warnings on products such as cigarettes, when it is not required by local legislation

● *employee safety* – accident and fatality rates at Third World subsidiaries of manufacturing companies often exceed those at home by a considerable margin

● *marketing* – e.g. misleading or unsubstantiated claims about products or failing to take into account the social impact of specific marketing approaches upon unsophisticated audiences. (The dangers of inadequate attention to the potential problems of marketing in the Third World are amply born out by the Nestle case.

More than a decade after the issue was 'settled' many people still associate Nestle primarily not with health and high quality foods, but with the death of Third World babies.)

• *pollution control* – some companies have taken advantage of laxer anti-pollution legislation in Third World countries to reduce production costs. However, the developing countries themselves now increasingly recognise that the environmental price they are paying to attract and keep these industries is too high. They too are tightening up their requirements. MNCs building new plants will therefore benefit from incorporating the most modern, effective pollution controls, on the grounds that it is cheaper to build these in at the design stage, than to add them later.

Case study: *Proctor and Gamble International*

US-based multinational Proctor and Gamble has operating companies in over 29 countries and has a clearly defined policy on how to conduct its business abroad.

The company's president, William Gurganus, discussed this policy at a conference on multinational citizenship during a convention of the US National Foreign Trade Council, explaining that each time Proctor and Gamble started business in a new country they have been guided by three general objectives:

Never to forget that Proctor and Gamble is a guest of that country.

It is bound by its laws and also obliged to do its best to blend the company's overall policies with local customs and practices.

In practical terms, this commits the company:

– to be sensitive and responsive to the social and economic conditions in the host country.

– to employ at all levels citizens of the host country who are qualified applicants

– to give all employees the opportunity to rise to higher positions not only in their own country, but also in other Proctor and Gamble organizations around the world

– to compete vigorously but fairly with local competitors. But to compete in ways which will lead these competitors to respect our integrity as well as our ability

– to avoid meddling in the politics of the host country

– to strive to achieve a reputable identity and not be looked upon as simply the branch of an American parent

– to pay good wages in line with responsible local practices in the community, in which it operates

– to establish easy channels of communication with each community and country so that each will have a better understanding of the action or inaction of the other.

Proctor and Gamble has listed its common stock on a number of foreign exchanges and regularly distributes translated versions of its annual report. If citizens of host countries want to own part of the business, they can often do so by buying Proctor and Gamble stock.

Case study: *The Body Shop*

The Body Shop has a very different philosophy from most companies. It sets out to source products in the Third World in an 'unpatronizing and unexploitative' manner, because it believes that encouraging local communities in developing countries to grow ingredients and make products for the company creates employment and trade. It also has a policy of paying the same wages, whatever country it operates in.

The Footsie Roller, a smooth wooden foot massager, is a good example of this policy. Here the company is working alongside the Boys' Town Trust, which cares for destitute children in southern India during their secondary school years. The boys are taught trades that enable them to earn a living when they return to their villages. Lathe workers aged from 16–20 make the footsie rollers from local fast growing wood. This initiative has developed into a new local industry in ten very poor villages.

In order not to ruin the local economy by flooding it with a mass of highly affluent teenagers, the Body Shop has arranged that the boys are paid directly only the going rate for the local labour market. The rest is held in trust until they leave the Boys' Town Trust. At that time, their share of the money is used to set each of them up in a trade – for example by buying each one a lathe or a pair of oxen and a plough.

The Body Shop has also set up an alternative papermaking project in Nepal, one of the poorest countries in the world. The Nepalese economy is based on fragile subsistence agriculture, now damaged by appalling deforestation.

Hand papermaking using lokta, a daphne shrub, dates from the 11th century. Recently the industry had been stripping too much daphne bark and was beginning to destroy the forests where it thrived. In response, the Nepalese government put a ceiling on daphne use. Papermaking declined. Whole villages were out of work.

Now, as part of the Body Shop project, workers are mixing alternative fibres such as banana, water hyacinth, bamboo and sugar cane with recycled daphne to make new papers, new jobs and new hopes.

Water hyacinth is a prolific weed, which chokes rivers in tropical regions. By harvesting it to make paper, you also clear the rivers. Banana trees flourish in Nepal. They grow to their full height in about 18 months and then produce fruit. The tree then collapses and the fibres rot away until a new shoot rises from the old root. Banana fibre can successfully be used with lokta, or on its own for papermaking purposes.

Mara Amats, consultant on the Body Shop's Third World projects points out: 'Too much daphne bark was being stripped for paper. There was no more work for the papermakers. I simply showed them that banana was an alternative. That's my job.'

The first papers arrived in the UK in early 1989. Customers can buy bags, notebooks, purses, wallets and pot pourris made from the new paper on many of Britain's high streets.

Says the Body Shop: 'Trade not aid entails a constant search for ways in which the company can use manufactured Third World products.' The company is investigating other projects in the Amazon basin with tribes living in the Xingu region. Its product development team is investigating nine materials including brazil nut, andiroba and breu branco, for a tropical rainforest range of cosmetics and toiletries. The company explains: '"The Body Shop's efforts to create markets for plants from tropical forests are intended to promote the economic independence of the forest people. They are the guardians of the forest and are the primary source of ideas for regenerating areas of forest that have already been degraded or cleared. It is almost impossible to predict what effect the emerging markets will have on patterns of land use in the tropical forests of Brazil. It is also very difficult to predict what reaction there will be from wealthy landowners and businesses when they see that 'their' resource base is being spread out amongst a minor, under-privileged sector of the rural population.

"The Body Shop will, however, do as much as possible to ensure that markets are carefully and preferentially directed to communities of forest people."'

Case study: *RTZ Corporation*

RTZ is a company that has received considerable criticism, particularly on environmental grounds, over the years. But the mining and manu-facturing conglomerate regards itself as a caring and responsible employer and has gone to great pains to establish exemplary employment conditions in its Third World subsidiaries, such as Namibia's Rossing Uranium Ltd. When the mine began production in 1976, the company was unable to find suitably-trained local labour. Most of the people in the area, seeking work at the mine, were unfamiliar with the industry. In addition, their educational levels were low and they were mainly illiterate and innu-merate. So Rossing had to train employees from an elementary level before it could productively employ them.

In 1979, Rossing established formal operator training, which has now been provided to some 1,200 operators. It also has a formal programe of continuous training so that people learn to do more skilled jobs, and a student programme to provide the company with future managers. Selected school leavers interested in a career with Rossing spend a year with the company, receiving bridging education in maths, science and English. During the year they also receive leadership training and broad exposure to the mine and its systems, as well as working within their chosen discipline. After completing the year they are sent to a university or technical college for degree or diploma courses in subjects such as management, engineering, accountancy and commerce. On qualifying, the graduate starts work at the mine. About 70 trainees are on the scheme at any one time.

In addition, the company constantly tests black employees with an eye to promotion. In the late eighties it promoted over 2,200 blacks. Rossing teaches English literacy to its employees and encourages them to strive for a degree or a diploma on correspondence courses.

At a national level, the company established the Rossing Foundation in 1978 to concentrate on providing adult education to a wide cross section of Namibians. It built an adult education centre, which offers courses in literacy, sewing, and three standards of English and German. It has donated language laboratories and computers to local schools and helped to build a primary school and a secondary school in the self contained community of Arandis. The company also sponsors Namibians to study in America and Britain on the condition that they return to their country afterwards.

Wherever possible, Rossing purchases goods and services inside Namibia. For example, it buys work clothes at the market price from a local women's co-operative.

Checklist
1. Do you have a written policy detailing standards of behaviour in host countries?
2. Do you actively reinvest profits in the host country?
3. Do you transfer technology to the developing world in line with its needs?
4. Do you place a heavy emphasis on training in Third World countries?
5. Do you attempt to work within the confines of the traditional culture?
6. Are standards of pollution control, safety, marketing and product safety common throughout your operations?

73

5.2 Human rights

Companies that operate in host countries with a poor human rights record have to be especially careful that they do not offend the international community to the detriment of their business.

Those US and European companies which pulled out of South Africa as a result of public pressure against apartheid took, for the most part, commercial decisions, based on the cost of loss of business elsewhere against the profits from their S. African operations. Many of the MNCs that remained have taken strong positions at the forefront of the practical fight against apartheid, providing models of how a non-discriminatory employer should behave.

These companies do not operate segregation; they pay above the supplemented living level and educate blacks in order to promote them into higher positions in the workforce. They refuse to use migrant or contract labour, give their workers fringe benefits such as pension schemes and health schemes and, in some cases help blacks to buy their own houses or at the very least rent family homes at reasonable rates.

Some recognise the unions, if they have been set up, and encourage them by providing special training for union officials. In areas where the union movement is weak, they set up councils, which give employees an official voice.

The serious problems for these companies arise when local legislation requires them to act in ways that contradict basic standards of human rights. The experience of most companies faced with this dilemma is that they first look for ways round the legislation, then, if that is not possible, ignore it in hopes that the host government will not make it an issue if they do not. To a considerable extent, experience in S. Africa has shown that this approach works. Significantly, the personnel management profession has been at the forefront of pushing the boundaries of apartheid-free practice in S. Africa.

If current political trends continue in S. Africa, they will presumably have an impact on companies' decisions over whether to reinvest in that country. But many of the underlying social problems will take decades (at least) to resolve and these companies must be aware that the human rights issues will remain on the agenda. Moreover, although S. Africa is the country where human rights abuses have most often caused dilemmas for businesses, it is far from the only country where companies have encountered such problems.

The value of the S. African experience is that it provides useful lessons for companies in how to deal with human rights conflict. Many companies investing in China, for example, had already been through the relevant thinking processes. As a result, their decisions to withdraw, either permanently or temporarily, were made rapidly, without lengthy public pressure.

A clear statement of company ethics – i.e. a code of international practice – is a key starting point for making judgements about appropriate behaviour. It not only gives local managers a touchstone, but allows the company to put its behaviour into an ethical or moral context to concerned audiences in other countries. The statement should examine, among other things, the conditions under which the company would no longer find it tenable to continue business operations within a country and how it would alleviate the human problems, such as job losses, which would result from a withdrawal under those circumstances.

Case study: *RTZ Corporation*

RTZ's Rossing subsidiary, one of the largest uranium mines in the world, has a clear human rights policy.

It states: 'Rossing's social contribution has also been important to Namibia. Steadfastly opposed to racial discrimination in the workplace and in the community as a whole, Rossing's practical example is followed by those organizations and people who wish to be part of an emergent Namibia.'

Trade unionism is not developed in Namibia, but Rossing has established a workers' council where employees can voice grievances and problems. The Rossing Council system has a two tier structure. It consists of five divisional committees at the lower level. In addition, a residential committee meets with relevant managers to discuss off site matters such as housing, transport and recreational facilities. The upper tier of Rossing Council meets at less frequent intervals with the general manager to discuss policy issues and matters affecting the interests of employees across all divisions. Among practical results for employees have been an extension on their personal health and accident insurance cover, changes to the design of new company houses and longer paid leave for low grade staff.

The council representatives receive training in their functions and duties. They have permanent representation on the company job evaluation grading committee, medical society and pension fund. In addition, they have the right to assist colleagues in disciplinary and grievance cases if requested to do by the persons concerned.

Case study: *Thorn-EMI*

Thorn-EMI, which currently runs several operations in South Africa, has a clear statement of opposition to apartheid and welcomes the progress currently being made to end it. It also endorses the CBI's reluctance to support general sanctions because 'we share their doubts about the effectiveness of such general sanctions for achieving that goal'.

Over the last few years the company has reduced its investment in South Africa, selling its rental business in December 1985, its engineering businesses in 1986 and another business, Kenwood, in 1989.

It publishes a written document explaining its operations in South Africa, where it states: 'No Thorn EMI company sells defence equipment to South Africa. Our electronics companies sell ticket machines and tubes which are used in diamond sorting equipment.'

Thorn allows no segregation at work. According to the company's document on South Africa, all employees are paid on a non-discriminatory basis at above average salary levels. The EC Code of Conduct published by the DTI in July 1986 states that 'pay based on the supplemented living level (SLL) for an average sized family must be considered the absolute minimum necessity', noting that there are five in an average family. Thorn-EMI Lighting in Johannesburg employs 110 blacks, only eight of whom are on the lowest wage, which is 15% above the SLL.

Thorn Lighting has also recognised and signed a recognition agreement with the multi-racial Radio and Television and Allied Workers Union and allows unions free recruiting access to staff.

Checklist
1. Does your company have a policy of equal employment opportunity, wherever it operates? Is it implemented?
2. Does your company have clear guidelines on how to react to human rights problems?

5.3 Lobbying

It seems ironical that the lobbying industry, which aims to influence legislation and ministerial decisions, should be faced with the threat that the parliaments of Westminster and Brussels will regulate its activities – and be unable to influence it. Unable to agree on self-regulation, the lobbyists are under increasing attack for their role in representing organizations and special interest groups.

The dilemma for companies lies in deciding when it is ethical and responsible to lobby, and when not. Clearly any business has a responsibility to represent its shareholders' interests, and that must include attempting to persuade government not to pass legislation that will damage the company's markets, or reduce its profits, for example. But what if the interests of the shareholders are directly opposed to those of the community?

Both the Public Relations Consultancy Association and the Institute of Public Relations have codes of conduct that include references to lobbying, but there are still a great many grey areas, where managers can only be guided by what they feel to be 'right'.

Charles Hendry, a former political advisor to government departments and now a senior consultant with Burson-Marsteller has observed these issues from both sides. He sees lobbying as a natural part of the marketing process and offers the following practical advice:

● *Responsible corporate lobbying comes from long-term under-standing.* Companies, which attempt to create relationships with MPs and senior Civil Servants only when they perceive a threat to their business, are less likely to succeed.

Long-term relationships allow MPs to understand the company and its industry and allow managers to understand how the legislative system works. Unethical behaviour is most likely to come from organizations which do not have this understanding.

● *Retaining an MP is not always the best way to influence legislation.* It is commonplace for a company to retain a member as its consultant and expect him or her to vote in the company's favour if a relevant issue arises in the House. The problem is, the retained MP often loses credibility, if he has a declared interest.

However, not all members' interests are declared. If an MP is retained by a PR consultancy, for example, the public does not know which issues he is really standing for. The Register of Members Interests will only list the consultancy and not its clients. Companies should consider whether they would be better to have an open relationship.

Another relevant issue to consider is conflict of interest. Hendry advises: 'If I was an MP I would not accept payment from any company within my constituency. I should be working for them anyway. If there is a conflict of interests, an MP should ensure that the constituency comes first.' He believes that select committee members should be particular who retains them, and that there should be a Register of Lobbyists, who would then have to make it clearer what they were doing.

- *Lobbying is not always the appropriate way to exert influence.*
  A company should:

- *establish what its need is.* Does it have to be done through a public affairs (lobbying) programme? Could advertising/PR achieve the same end?

'Influence the public first and then parliament,' says Hendry. 'The best lobbying is often good practice. For example, The Body Shop has a huge amount of good publicity. It does not need to lobby MPs about animal testing because they are already aware of the importance of the issue thanks to media articles and consumer campaigns.'

- *ensure it is not lobbying for the impossible* – for example, a lowering of interest rates when high interest rates are part of the Chancellor's long term economic strategy

- *if it does retain an MP, it should not concentrate its efforts on one* – far better to establish a body of opinion in the house. Give those you do retain clear guidelines on behaviour, preferably in writing.

- *be careful not to ally itself with pressure groups.* Says Hendry, 'They often suceed by scaring people with select snippets of information and the government can be slow to check out all the facts to get the whole picture. If a company is known to take on unhelpful causes the relevant people will be less willing to talk to you. In addition, government is wary of pressure groups, because however it responds the pressure group says 'It is too little too late'.

- *if it is doing something well, write and inform the members.* They have to be made aware of what is happening. Gain friends, so that in the event of a takeover bid, for example, your company is already highly regarded.

- *be open* – too much secrecy and lying will destroy your case – be prepared to answer awkward questions and explain what you are doing or you will be misunderstood

- *treat separate parties differently, but evenhandedly.*

Case study: *British Airways*

According to Hendry, BA is 'wonderful' at maintaining contact with parliament.

It regularly holds presentations and entertains select commitees. It is active at both party conferences. Through such techniques, it makes sure that MPs have a high background awareness of the company's needs.

This pays off when threats appear. For example, when American access to British airports was an issue, BA already had a firm body of support in the house.

It is worth noting that BA doesn't retain a member. It doesn't need to. According to Hendry, if it had only started campaigning when disadvantageous legislation was mooted in the house, the chances of success would have been negligible.

Case study: *Industry and Parliament Trust*

The Industry and Parliament Trust (IPT) was formed by 11 companies in 1977 to bridge the understanding gap between industry and MPs. The gap arises in part from differences in objectives, but also from the fact that very few MPs have direct experience of business management.

IPT's main objectives are:
– to enable members of both houses of parliament and British members of the European parliament to widen their experience in, and increase their knowledge of, industry
– to improve the understanding of industrial managers about the problems of parliament in dealing with matters affecting industry. The trust, which is an educational charity, is strictly non-partisan. It is open to parliamentarians of all parties. It is not a lobbying organization.

Member companies finance the trust, which runs fellowship programmes designed to give MPs an insight into industry. The MPs volunteer to spend about 25 days in one year with a major company. They get the chance to see how business functions from the inside and gain a greater understanding of the constraints business operates under.

Key points of the trust's fellowship programme are:
– to provide a bird's eye view of the company's business objectives, its strategies for achieving them and the institutional framework for implementing those strategies
– to give an appreciation of the scope of business operations from grass roots activities through management and functional supporting structures
– to show how a professionally managed group tackles planning, budgeting, investment appraisal, overseas expansion and other decision making activities
– to involve the MP in the processes of management so that they can see at first hand how decisions are reached

– to create a dialogue with MPs on problems of industrial relations and employee participation and give them the opportunity to see union consulation/employee participation in action

– to improve MPs' understanding of the extent to which government strategies and legislation affect the business

– to give business a better understanding of how the parliamentary system works

– to show businessmen how MPs see companies

Some parliamentarians enjoy the fellowship so much that they come back for another dose. In this case, the trust tries to arrange them 'post-graduate' facilities with small businesses.

With the increase in small business activity over recent years, the trust sees it as a major objective to involve firms of all sizes in its activities. To help the politicians gain a complete perspective of British industry, the trust encourages them to take on short term courses of four or five days with smaller companies.

Control and Readout, a small business member provided a four day post-graduate programme for one MP. This consisted of:

Day one:

am – Introduction to company organization, management philosophy, style, history and future plans, government aids and legislation and how they affect the smaller company, effects of rapid technological change on company practices, and the personal objectives of major shareholders and directors.

pm – spent with junior directors, plus tour of the plant and confidential discussions with office and shop floor personnel.

Day two:

Detailed session with the chairman, mainly on financial matters, but also covering relationships with the local authority. A visit to the bank for wider discussions.

Day three:

This took place a few weeks later and consisted of a session to inform employees about the workings of parliament and the legislative process, followed by a private meeting with the chairman for a frank report by the MP on his impression of the company.

Day four:

After a further interval, the MP returned for an update, and to check on projects and answer queries.

Checklist
1. Does your company have a clearly defined policy on lobbying?
2. Would an outside observer consider your lobbying activities as open, fair and justifiable?

6 Responsibility towards the broader community

The concept that companies have responsibilities towards the community at large is far from new. Corporate philanthropy was a burning issue for the Victorian entrepreneurs, for example. In his book *Enlightened Entrepreneurs*, Ian Campbell Bradley explores the lives of 10 Victorian businessmen. Although many of their policies on community care might now be regarded as paternalistic, they were the forerunners of today's social responsibility movement.

In the 1800s, the Nonconformist Colmans, still famous today for their mustard, established provident funds, clothing funds and compulsory accident insurance. Colman's wife Caroline launched a works kitchen which provided cheap food and drink. Prices covered the cost of raw materials. Preparation and cooking costs were met by the company. Caroline herself acted as 'lady superintendent' and specified that they should open at 5.45 am in the morning for tea and coffee for workers who had a long walk to work.

Boots is to the retail trade what Colmans is to mustard. Jesse Boot's attitude to the workforce was autocratic but beneficient. Boot was involved with several philanthropic projects in Nottingham, where the chain first started in the mid 1800s.

In 1908 he established 11 homes, in memory of his daughter Dorothy, for veterans of the Crimean war and the Indian Mutiny. In the same year he gave much of the money to rebuild the Albert Hall, a centre for temperance meetings and Wesleyan Methodist services in the town. He also gave £5,000 for an organ in the hall, provided that popular recitals would be held there every Saturday afternoon with cheap seats so all could attend.

Quakers George and Richard Cadbury, founders of the chocolate manufacturers, built a model village in Bourneville, Birmingham, for staff and the local community. They bought the land because they were determined to prevent speculators moving into the area and putting up cramped sub-quality houses for their workers.

In their village, a pedestrian could walk from one end of the estate to the other without leaving parkland and each house had a large garden.

Bourneville was used as a showplace and helped create a much greater interest in town planning. George Cadbury continued his interest in the issue by establishing a lectureship in civic design and town planning at Birmingham University.

Why should today's companies exhibit this concern?

The most forceful arguments come from the companies themselves. Thorn-EMI has a well-established giving policy and involves itself in everything from charitable donations through to educational sponsorship and training, giving over 0.5 per cent of UK pre-tax profits through its corporate responsibility programme. Explains chairman Colin Southgate:

'No business exists in a vacuum. At Thorn EMI we are conscious of the influence our businesses have on communities throughout the UK both locally and nationally. We recognise that 'business' is not only a matter of serving our customers well – it brings with it responsibilities to the communities where Thorn-EMI businesses operate.

If a community as a whole flourishes, the individual members of that community tend to flourish too. A flourishing community is one which is prosperous, healthy, educated, inventive and which cares for the less fortunate. All these aspects are related and any company which wishes to make a meaningful contribution to the community, as Thorn-EMI does, will try to address these aspects.

It is in Thorn EMI's interests to be part of a flourishing community. The more prosperous a community, the more it will buy our goods and services. This is mutually beneficial, since the more we can improve our financial performance, the more we can give back to the community.'

IBM's community investment policy states three clear reasons for its detailed strategy:
● to contribute to the economic and social well-being of the communities in which we operate, thereby helping to make them better places for us to do business
● to be recognised by government, customers, business partners and our own employees as a leader in effective and enlightened corporate community involvement
● to improve morale and motivation of our employees through

their awareness of, support for and involvement in the company's activities.

Kingfisher's written community involvement policy is in a similair vein but shorter:

'We believe a healthy business needs a healthy community. Kingfisher companies are committed to helping improve the quality of life in communities throughout the UK. We direct our special efforts towards charities, organizations and projects which share our concerns, and which benefit the people who are our employees and customers. And we concentrate on key areas such as health, education, crime prevention, enterprise and homelessness. Priority goes to pioneering projects, which help people develop new skills or gain new experiences, and to activities, which give scope for our employees to become involved.'

A strong common theme running through many of these corporate statements is that involvement in community affairs is of mutual benefit to both the company and the community. It is not enough for a company to exist in harmony with the community – it must also have a strong interest in its development. Having made the philosophical commitment to community involvement, there is no shortage of opportunities – quite the opposite. The problem comes in finding a structured approach for both the community and the long term shareholders.

A good starting point is to classify activities into broad categories upon which the organization can make decisions as to the extent to which it should become involved. It can then sub-divide these categories where it believes it should become involved into areas, upon which it can make more specific decisions.

We suggest here five such broad categories:
- corporate and staff giving
- secondment
- sponsorship
- education and schools liaison
- small business development.

As with most classifications of social responsibiity issues, there may be overlap between these categories.

6.1 The giving company

In 1988, British companies gave an estimated £135 million to charitable causes – more than a third more than four years before. British Telecommunications topped the league chart of community contributors with donations of over £11,082,000, National Westminster Bank and Barclays Bank coming second and third with £9,700,000 and £7,306,000 respectively. But the ranks of frequent givers also include a growing number of small and medium-sized companies.

But why do companies give? According to *A Guide To Company Giving*, published by the Directory of Social Change, keeping up with similiar businesses is a common reason. Other companies like to give to charities, whose activities will benefit their business sector – for example, pharmaceutical companies sponsoring cancer research, computer companies helping spread computer literacy or retail businesses sponsoring crime prevention projects. Some firms simply want to be seen as good neighbours and will support charities where they have branches – banks, retail chains and building societies are especially fond of this form of giving. The payoffs come in improved recruitment and, for service businesses, such as hotels, enhanced market awareness. A lot of organizations believe that employee fund-raising initiatives encourage team-work that benefits the businesses, too. Others have schemes to donate money to charities that employees are involved in, thereby encouraging good relations between staff and management.

As the benefits become clearer, so companies are taking more steps to ensure that they receive the credit due for their good works. A community affairs director from a major bank said: 'In recent years the government has been demanding that we take a more responsible role in the community. We have always taken on that role but now we are publicizing it more.'

Case study: *The Per Cent Club*

The Per Cent Club is a group of some 300 leading companies which are committed to making a significant contribution to the communities in which they operate. More than half the members are in *The Times'* Top 500.

Launched in 1986, the qualification for membership is the contribution of no less than half a per cent of pre-tax (UK) profits to the community. Companies may donate to charitable organizations, job creation initiatives, training schemes, local economic development as well as education, the arts or music.

6.1.1 *A helping cheque*

High profile companies receive hundreds of requests for donations every year. A filtering and decision-making system is therefore essential. Typical systems involve the following:

1) *A written document stating priorities* gives the company a formal reason for accepting or rejecting requests. The giving policy document should also specify the sort of funding you are going to undertake. Many corporate donors will not give money towards core funding. Others prefer to give money to a small project that can be closely monitored. Others, such as Allied Dunbar, are willing to hand over large sums of money to help set up charity organisations in the hope that once the charity is successful, other companies will take over the funding.

2) *A vetting system*

Once a company has decided on the type of funding it will give, it must then work out a way of deciding whether candidate charities are going to be able to use donations effectively. In early 1990, many large and experienced corporate donors got their fingers burnt when the organisation 'War on Want' went bankrupt.

Some companies send their employees to the charity in question to vet it. Other firms audit the accounts and study how much money is going to the people the charity is supposed to help before making a decision. Other companies just opt for large charities such as the Great Ormond Street Wishing Well Appeal, safe in the knowledge that their money is in professional hands.

Some corporate donors demand that the organisation is not an enabling charity, like the World Wildlife Fund, but actually does the work.

In picking a charity, donors usually like to ensure that they have not chosen a similar cause to their competitors, otherwise the business value of the philanthropy will be reduced. So, for example, each bank has its own preferences. National Westminster supports the World Wildlife Fund, while Barclays supports the Royal Society for Protection of Birds.

Once you have selected and vetted a charity, it is important to allocate responsibility for keeping up to date with what it is doing. You should also let your employees know you are supporting it and why – for example through articles in the company newsletter.

Case study: *British Telecom*

British Telecom is one of the most generous corporate donors in the UK. In its company mission statement British Telecom pledges: 'to make a fitting contribution to the community in which we conduct our business'. The programme is led by a board level committee.

BT is one of the few companies which operates in every street throughout the UK. Each district office has its own independent community programme and may call on the centre for additional funding to ensure local needs are met.

The programme has five main areas of activity: action for the disabled customer, charities, community action, education and non-commercial sponsorship.

Action for Disabled Customers was launched in 1984 to reassure disabled people and the public of the company's concern for the needs of this minority. Its main thrust is to maintain and enhance products and services for disabled and elderly people. The action group keeps the disabled informed of the products available and publishes its own guide to equipment and services for disabled customers.

British Telecom has given over part of its Dundee premises to a disabled information centre. It also supports the Wolverhampton Resource Centre for Disabled People, which provides employment training, and visits local businesses to educate them about the positive aspects of employing people with disabilities.

BT's sponsorship for the disabled community includes funding the Royal National Institute for the Deaf's Text Users Help Scheme. The scheme helps people who use the deaf text facility over the telephone to pay the resulting larger phone bills.

In an entirely different sphere, the company has funded the setting up of a new company, Hansoff Communications, which provides cheap communication aids for the severely disabled. Hansoff itself is staffed by the disabled.

BT gives money to a wide range of national and local charities including those for medical research, the environment, national heritage and the Arts. Charities funding medical research or the provision of medical facilities are given high priority, particularly if they accord with company policy on occupational health. For example, BT has been promoting a 'Look after your Heart' campaign, so top management also decided to give money for research into heart disease.

The company has also given large donations to major hospital appeals such as Great Ormond Street, the Royal Marsden and the Help Hammersmith Cancer Campaign at the Hammersmith Hospital.

Crime prevention is not a major priority for BT's charitable support, although the chairman is patron of the Suzy Lamplugh Trust, which advises people how to avoid the risks of violence and aggression in the workplace and public places.

Most of Telecom's efforts are expended in the UK but some money is set aside for Third World projects, especially for longer term schemes to help areas affected by drought and famine.

Case study: *Allied Dunbar Assurance*

Allied Dunbar is one of the leaders in the field of corporate giving with a £2 million charitable programme and one of the biggest staff charity pay roll schemes in the country.

Sir Mark Weinberg, chairman, co-founded Business in the Community's Per Cent Club with United Biscuits' Sir Hector Laing in 1986. The company gives $1\frac{1}{4}\%$ of pre-tax profits to charity. This is over twice the qualifying amount for the Per Cent Club. This came to £937,000 in 1990.

The company has defined a set of principles which underlie its giving policies. Overall, it aims to support practical social welfare projects, but it has six guiding principles to help decide who to help.

Firstly, Allied Dunbar focuses on a limited geographical area. Secondly, it aims to support projects where its own donation will produce a knock on effect, i.e. where the grant will help an organization create a model, which can be replicated elsewhere or will help it attract funds from statutory organizations. Thirdly, the company prefers to back people rather than causes in the belief that success depends on the effectiveness of the people involved. Fourthly, Allied Dunbar tends to give larger grants to fewer organizations. This way chosen projects have more time to concentrate on development and consolidation. Fifthly, the community affairs department tries to remain flexible to the changes in society and to the charities which tackle these. The aim is to develop policies and procedures, which meet the charities' priorities and perception of needs rather than the company's. Allied Dunbar particularly recognises that it is often necessary to guarantee core costs, such as salaries.

Jerry Marston, deputy community affairs manager points out: 'Most companies have an angle when it comes to giving. They ask if they can have a van painted in their colours or the company logo on a charity's annual report. That is not our policy.'

He added: 'The intention was never to link charity work with company business. The Allied Dunbar Charitable Trust was established to ensure that independence.'

In line with the corporate giving policy, about one fifth of Allied Dunbar's donations are concentrated around Swindon where the company has its head office. The Trust, which has been running for over 18 years, funds six major initiatives.

The Community Initiatives policy gave over £107,000 in 1989 and aims to support practical services for the social welfare of people.

The company also has an Employment Promotion policy. Since 1987 this has given over £300,000 to support enterprise development training and support to the unemployed in Swindon.

Another noteworthy initiative is Action on Disability and Development (ADD), which was set up by the company in 1985 and given support of £500,000. ADD's aim is to work with self help groups for people with a disability in the Third World and to link up with similar groups in the U.K.

The company also has a special projects policy to respond to projects of outstanding excellence, which do not fall within its clearly defined objectives. Around £96,000 was given out in 1989 under this scheme.

The dedicated and cohesive social responsibility policy has had enormous benefits. Marston explains: 'The company's work in this field has made it more than pre-eminent. We get positioned on corporate donors lists alongside companies 20 or 30 times our size. We are frequently asked to speak at national and international conferences.'

The company tries to make sure that it does not take over the role relinquished by the state. Says Marston: 'We feel very uncomfortable taking over what was previously a state role. If you look at areas such as TECs, CTCs and the NHS you can see that the state is trying to roll back the public sector.' Where it does, as with the problems resulting from ill-coordinated closures of mental hospitals, it trys to ensure that donations are matched by local authority support.

For example, in 1987 Allied Dunbar's Charitable Trust undertook to donate at least £1 million over five years to help sufferers from schizophrenia and their relatives, many of whom had no access to public-sector supported facilities such as day care centres, work schemes, accommodation and respite care.

Marston explains that the charity schemes give staff a sense of common purpose and provide a team spirit within their own communities. People are more inclined to stay with a company that shows it is interested in issues beyond making money, he claims, adding: 'We use our charitable activity to advertise for staff with slogans such as "Working for Allied Dunbar is not only good for your conscience, it is also good for your career." We get more response from these than from normal adverts, so it clearly has benefits.'

The company also has a policy promoting more effective management of charities. Under this, it has established an Open University diploma course in 'Managing Voluntary and Non-profit Enterprises'.

Case study: *Kingfisher plc*

In 1988/89, Kingfisher's business and its employees contributed over £600,000 to a wide range of community projects.

A further £1.8 million was raised for Comic Relief by the sale of red noses through the Woolworths stores.

Kingfisher is a leading supporter of Business in the Community and has recently helped set in motion a new BiC initiative 'Women's Enterprise and Training' aimed at making more companies aware of women's potential in business. With two thirds of its workforce women, Kingfisher is especially keen to see their potential fully realised.

Kingfisher's support included boosting the campaign with professional publicity and sponsoring a booklet and the launch day. It also funds the Greater Opportunities for Women (GROW) initiative which is part of the Women's Economic Development Initiative.

GROW is a six month pilot project which aims to set up a database and produce a range of leaflets to help women in the West Midlands who are thinking of returning to work or changing their work arrangements. It aims to identify and inform women of local opportunities to upgrade and change their job, to obtain or update skills to go into paid employment or to start up and run their own businesses successfully. Kingfisher believes this information is desperately needed, because women returners often have to overcome a lack of self confidence which creates problems not only in terms of thinking about returning to work, but in terms of practical issues such as arranging childminding and domestic constraints.

Kingfisher explains its strong interest in giving to anti-crime initiatives: 'Companies have only recently started to look at how much crime costs them, and to extend their community programmes into the field of crime prevention. Crime is one of the biggest threats to the wellbeing of the community. It is often the cause of intense personal distress, disrupts people's lives and destroys the sense of security and trust which is vital to all community life. People have a right to feel safe when they are out shopping. We are one of Britain's largest retailers, and we believe we have a special responsibility to the customers who shop at our B&Q, Comet, Superdrug and Woolworths' stores.'

One of the reasons for Kingfisher's interest is that the company feels it has a duty to protect its 55,000 staff, who are often the victims of crime. In 1988, over 75 people working for Kingfisher companies were assaulted and needed hospital treatment. Many others suffered minor attacks, which still caused distress and shock. One manager at B&Q was stabbed in the neck as he chased a thief out of a store.

The financial costs are easier to quantify. The retail industry loses over £1.5 billion a year through crime, a high proportion of this due to shoplifting and other forms of theft. Security costs are inevitably reflected in prices.

Kingfisher believes that crime should no longer be left solely to the police to deal with and that businesses have a special role to play in crime prevention. They can lend their management skills and organizational ability as well as financial resources. For example, store managers can sit on crime prevention panels.

So, along with many other companies, Kingfisher now supports Crime Concern, which was launched in 1988 to promote general awareness of crime prevention. Kingfisher has used in-house expertise to advise the organization on points for action in business, sponsored a crime prevention booklet for schools, and one of the company's senior executives is a member of Crime Concern's board. In addition, with Crime Concern it has set up four pilot schemes around Britain to teach children the practical challenge of crime prevention and protection. Kingfisher is giving £20,000 to the project. Called Crucial Crew: The Kingfisher Junior Citizen Award Scheme, it aims to help children to avoid becoming crime victims, to develop good citizenship and to understand the role of the police and other emergency services. Crucial Crew is based on a competition consisting of a course of real life scenes which the children go round in pairs. They are evaluated on their reactions to problems presented in each scene. On completion they are given a certificate and a Crucial Crew T-shirt. Among other initiatives in this area, Kingfisher supported the CBI Crime Concern Business and Crime Initiative which produced the report 'Crime, Managing the business risk' on which a business and crime conference was based.

The company also sponsored a conference with the organisation, Victim Support, to raise awareness of how employers cope with employee crime victims.

Case study: *Midas Construction Ltd*

Midas Construction Limited, part of Devon-based Midas Construction Group, found an innovative way of combining business with giving to help a local school.

The story starts when Devon County Council awarded this medium sized company the contract to carry out alterations and extensions to Honiton Littletown Primary School.

Because of the alterations, the pre-school nursery, which had originally been housed in the school, had to be re-sited.

To solve the problem, Devon County Council agreed to give the school a mobile classroom as a nursery as long as the school paid for preparing the site.

Midas Construction responded flexibly when the governors approached it for the necessary work. The company agreed to do the additional labour, crane in the new building and contribute £500 towards funds.

Mr. Roy Cook, headmaster of the school said: 'Midas have kept the cost of the work down to a minimum. We have worked together on the school site in harmony. And then to find that the directors of Midas responded to my request for financial assistance with a cheque for £500 was overwhelming.'

Case study: *Trusthouse Forte plc*

Trusthouse Forte, one of the UK's largest hotel and catering companies, provides financial help to groups within a community that are improving, conserving and preserving the environment.

The Community Chest launched by THF in 1984 and organised by the Conservation Foundation, awards monthly grants of betweeen £100 and £1,000 to local environmental projects throughout the UK.

Since 1984, the Community Chest has helped restore a vintage double-decker bus, re-seed village greens, create school wildlife gardens, plant trees, restore church steeples and transform acres of wasteland into community gardens.

Groups who apply are judged by an independent panel of judges, headed by TV presenter and naturalist, David Bellamy. Once a group is awarded a grant, the Conservation Foundation puts it in touch with a local Trusthouse Forte hotel or restaurant to organise a cheque presentation.

Checklist

1. Does your company have a clear, written policy on corporate giving, setting out key priorities?
2. Do you vet charities against clear criteria?
3. Do you have both national and local budgets?
4. Do you monitor how the charity applies your donation?
5. Do you seek out charities, which meet your community objectives, other than wait for them to come to you?
6. Is your company a member of the Per Cent Club?

6.1.2 *Giving in kind*

Cash is only one of the resources a company can provide to help community initiatives.

Within the corporate environment are vast stores of equipment and technical know-how, from word-processing, desk top publishing and printing equipment, to jobbing workshops for maintenance. There may also be buildings, which can be loaned to the community outside of working hours for social functions, training, or exhibitions. Almost every facility a company has could potentially be of value in the community, at very little cost or risk – if only someone takes the trouble to seek appropriate opportunities.

Some companies, which produce and sell office equipment loan, give or – more frequently – sell it at reduced rates to bona fide voluntary organisations or to schools.

One of the first steps companies can take is to conduct a regular survey of corporate resources. Among the questions to ask are:

● What machinery or office equipment do we have that is no longer used?

● What machinery or scientific instrumention do we use, but could make available on a temporary basis to voluntary organisations? (For example, small businesses often have contracts with photocopier suppliers, based on minimum monthly volume. Giving any spare volume to a local charity costs nothing except paper, which the charity itself can supply.)

● Do we have spare office space/premises we no longer use, but don't want to rent out/sell?

All these questions the company ought to be asking for its own benefit anyway. Usage of equipment is important in determining the degree of waste in capital resources, and may lead to the hiring out of spare capacity in some cases. The storage of unwanted equipment may be tying up capital in the most unproductive way and using valuable space as well.

A resources survey may also point out poor usage of office or workshop space. If this can neither be used to good effect nor let to an outside organisation, it is likely to be an invaluable gift to a charity even on a temporary basis. The biggest fixed overhead of many charities is the space they place their chairs and filing cabinets in.

It can also be helpful to request all managers to check with the appeals committee before throwing out any obsolete equipment, or even partially damaged equipment that could be repaired by someone with the time. A desk minus a leg, an ancient manual typewriter, or a pile of paper with an outdated letter heading are all likely to be of use to some voluntary organization. For example, when communications company, The ITEM Group, replaced its computer systems, it donated some of the outdated computers to a charity. The cost to the company was nil; the value to the charity considerable.

Case study: *British Rail*

British Rail gave 11 building units to new firms in a disused train crew depot as part of Lincoln Enterprise Agency's innovation centre. This was a partnership between the city and the County Council, the Manpower Services Commission and the local enterprise agency.

Case study: *IBM*

During 1989 IBM offered 100 fully configured personal computer systems to charities and community organizations nominated by employees. Successful charities were chosen on the basis of their relevance to IBM's community investment priorities, the length and extent of the employees' involvement and the charities' ability to use the system effectively and advantageously.

IBM has also given equipment to the United Kingdom Support Centre for People with Disabilities, established at IBM Warwick in late 1988. This is the flagship of IBM UK's information technology (IT) and disabiliity activities. The centre gives specialist and technical advice on how IT can meet the needs of the disabled.

Other projects involving equipment donation include one at the Open University, which uses IBM PS/2 screen readers to support blind students, SpeechViewer trials at the National Hospitals Centre for Speech Sciences in London, a PS/2 project to develop software for people with head injuries at the ACE Centre in Oxford and a PC-based note taking and transcription system for the deaf at Bristol University.

In addition, IBM offers a special price scheme to people with disabilities and non-profit making or government organizations established to work on their behalf.

Charity customers can buy equipment at 40% discount from IBM list prices. The scheme covers the complete Personal System/2 range, including a selection of accessories and attachments, software and networking and communications equipment. It also covers post-warranty maintenance agreements.

Case study: *Allied Dunbar Assurance plc*

Recognising that money is rarely the only commodity a charity needs, the Report of the Allied Dunbar Charitable Trust for 1987 says in a statement of the principles underlying its policies: 'Wherever appropriate we are keen to work with charities to provide a package of support which will help them make more effective use of the finance they receive. This can include technical advice, management support, equipment, access to company premises and publicity.'

Under ALPHA (Allied Professional Help and Advice) the company loans out people from its accounts, premises, systems, personnel and marketing departments to help charities. For example, training staff from the personnel department have established a management training and development consultancy programme with five major local Swindon charities.

Allied Dunbar also offers a free design and printing service which is available to Swindon charities. During 1989, the service carried out over 30 different jobs.

The company regularly allows charities access to its head office in Swindon for special meetings, seminars and annual general meetings. Groups who have made use of the facility include Drug Link, the Samaritans and Wiltshire County education department.

The staff of the community affairs department give advice and information on fund-raising. They maintain an extensive library, sit on appeal committees, produce regular bulletins and write, print and distribute free of charge, publications like 'Pennies from Heaven' (a guide to sources of funds for small and medium sized charities) and 'Do's and Don'ts of Applying to Charitable Trusts'.

Case study: *Coverdale Organisation*

Smaller companies sometimes lead the field in finding new methods of giving.

The Coverdale Organisation is a management consultancy and training service employing about 100 people. It runs subsidised consultancy and training courses for worthwhile courses in the community.

The programme is run by Coverdale in the Community, Coverdale's community affairs agency, and is an extension of its policy 'contribution in action'. Rather than donate sums of money to charity, it prefers to donate skills.

The leadership Development Programme is Coverdale's newest and most ambitious scheme. A bursary programme, it helps disabled people develop management skills through training over a year. The content of the training is determined by the bursary winners in partnership with Coverdale's consultants. Teamwork, leadership and negotiation form the core framework. Midland Bank is supporting the scheme by offering access to its own in-house training programmes.

The scheme is a prime example of how businesses can work together for the benefit of each other and the community at large.

The programme is unusual, because it gives skills directly to disabled people rather than to the charities that represent them.

In the first year, three people were offered a place on the programme.

Midland Bank was so impressed by one candidate that it created a fourth place for her, on a Midland bursary.

The Coverdale places are called 'The Brisenden Bursaries', in memory of Simon Brisenden, a writer on disability issues, who died in May 1989. Simon was one of the first disabled people to attend a Coverdale course.

The managing director of Disability Matters Ltd attended a Managers and Professionals course in September 1989 as part of the Coverdale in the Community Programme. He explains in the June 1990 edition of the Coverdale Review that he has been able to pass on what he has learnt to other disabled people and incorporate many of the ideas into his own work. In addition, other team members, who had often had very little contact with disabled people, had the chance to learn more about disability.

Checklist
1. Do you do a resources audit regularly?
2. What do you do with spare equipment/space/premises? Could you give them to a needy charity in the area?
3. Have you allocated somebody to monitor resources and suggest recipient charities?
4. Could you loan equipment to a charity to help it with essentials such as publicity or accounts?

6.1.3 *Employee giving*

Companies that encourage their staff to raise money for their favourite charities through raffles, sponsored walks or sponsored diets reap the rewards in improved motivation and team spirit and local reputation.

Some companies run 'give as you earn' schemes to help employees make giving to charity part of their regular expenditure. They merely sign an agreement assigning a proportion of salary to a charity. But this type of scheme has its disadvantages, as a major retailer explains, 'It is not very popular. It does not encourage team spirit. The money is just taken from your wage packet and you don't see anything tangible. It is much better to do raffles or sponsored events, which involve staff getting to know people from other sections of the business.'

Companies can also show their encouragement for employee involvement in charity initiatives by pinning requests for volunteers on the noticeboard. Staff who volunteer to work at a charity in their spare time will have an inside knowledge of its activities. When the company is looking for worthy causes to support, employees can then put their charity forward.

Another way of ensuring employee involvement is to ask staff to nominate the charities they would like the company to support on the grounds that they are more likely to put more effort into fund-raising activities for these charities.

Similarly, some companies have found they can achieve objectives such as quality improvement or workplace safety by donating incentives to employee-chosen charities instead of to individuals.

Case study: *Barclays Bank*

Barclays Bank has over 3000 branches and outlets all over the British Isles and staff at these outposts make a major contribution to local and national charities through their own fund raising activities. The bank matches staff fund raising pound for pound which gives fund raisers an added incentive to organise fancy dress days and sponsored darts events.

Case study: *ICI*

When ICI Pharmaceuticals, Macclesfield had won major awards in the past, it usually recognised employees' efforts by presenting them with a token, such as an inscribed pen. More recently, however, it celebrated receiving the Queen's Award for Industry by asking employees how they would like to use the money. They suggested donating two ambulances, costing £28,000, to Community Transport Macclesfield Borough, a charity that operates transport services for elderly and disabled people.

Plant management had looked for a project that was related to health care and was visible so everybody could feel proud of the gift.

The retired employee who suggested the idea is now treasurer of the charity. He originally approached ICI for £1,000 towards running the fleet.

ICI gained coverage in the national press, and a more motivated workforce. The ICI venture is the first time any of the 2,688 winners have put the award to such imaginative use.

Case study: *National Sleep-Out Week*

Some causes provide an opportunity for companies and employees to both raise cash for charity and to publicise the problem the charity addresses. National Sleep-Out Week and a variety of smaller, similar events aim 'to give people an insight into the miseries of homelessness, whilst being able to actively do something to help'. Kingfisher's sponsored sleep-out in cardboard boxes on the streets of London in Spring 1990 raised £10,000 towards the St Mungo Housing Association's £500,000 target to set up five new hostels for the homeless.

Explained corporate affairs director, Nigel Whittaker: 'We like to contribute to events where we think our help will make a difference. I believe helping is not just simply signing a cheque, and we encourage our staff to get involved wherever they can.'

Checklist
1. Do you allow staff time off each year to help their charity?
2. Have you got a 'Give as You Earn' scheme?
3. Do you consult your staff about what charities you donate to?
4. Do you hold sponsorship events to raise funds for charity?
5. Did your company have a collecting box for any of the major recent national appeals? Was somebody nominated to take it around for a week?
6. Does your company match employee giving?

6.2 Secondment

Seconding employees is an accepted way for companies to loan charities their most valuable resources – people, and their management skills. As the concept grew in the early 1970s, a number of businesses came together to form the Action Resource Centre (ARC) to help and advise companies in making secondment work. ARC is now the main clearing house for secondment, although many companies organise their own schemes. More recently companies have recognised the value of secondment as a means of developing management trainees.

Secondment has a number of advantages. The secondee gains an opportunity to:
1. Develop previously unused skills
2. Cultivate an interest in social issues
3. Come into contact with a different way of life, organization structure, values and ideals and learn to get the best out of it
4. Use their initiative

The charity gains:
1. A professional it could not otherwise afford
2. The chance to learn new business techniques
3. A contact that may be useful later
4. Extra manpower

The company gets:
1. Fast and challenging development of management or the

opportunity to ease valued employees into retirement
2. General approval from employees and the broader community
3. An opportunity to influence community planning
4. Understanding of the community through direct contact of secondees

The amount of time spent on secondment varies. Some secondees have acted as advisors to charities on an ad hoc basis, some have spent a two year stint working with a voluntary organization before retiring; some have worked with a charity on long term secondment in mid career; and some companies, such as major accountancy firms, use secondment as a means of broadening the knowledge and scope of trainees.

The result is a stream of valuable professional resources being directed into the community. Through ARC's new scheme 'Lawyers in the Community' lawyers are being brought onto the management committees of local organisations. City lawyers have been recruited to join such committees in Tower Hamlets, Hackney and Southwark in Greater London. A similar scheme applies to accountants.

ARC also encourages companies to allow voluntary staff from charities on internal training courses. Community organizations are often so desperately short of professional and management skills that ARC advocates that firms second people with training skills, who can pass on their knowledge and have a lasting effect on their placement organization.

The secondee's return to the company must be handled with care. Early experience with secondment found that instead of increasing employee motivation as the companies had expected, in many cases it increased the secondees' dissatisfaction with their jobs and their employers. After working in a broader environment, where they can make decisions on their own initiative, and from having a project of their own, they found it hard to readjust to an organized, disciplined and bureaucratic atmosphere. Other secondees have come back to find there was no longer a meaningful job waiting for them. They had little choice but to look for alternative employment.

Still others have enjoyed their secondment so much that they decided not to return. Marks and Spencers lost a personnel officer a few years ago after she did a stint for Oxfam. And IBM in the UK had to relinquish a senior manager who was so taken with a secondment project that he stayed on as director at one third of his previous pay.

These companies learnt that the secondee needed to be kept in touch with his or her former department throughout their absence and that secondment should be viewed on all sides as a significant opportunity to gain subsequent promotion.

Case study: *IBM*

IBM UK has run a secondment programme since 1970. To date nearly 200 employees have been loaned out for periods ranging from one month to three years. The objective of the programme is to make a contribution to the community through the transfer of skills, while at the same time contributing to the career development of IBM employees.

The programme is open to employees from all levels of the company, who have three years service. Although the majority of secondments have been to traditional charities, a growing number have been to enterprise agencies, which help establish small businesses. Attachments have also been arranged to universities and government departments. More recently, some 50 civil servants and academics have joined IBM on inward secondments, bringing different skills, expertise and perspective.

Among typical secondments, an IBM technical support manager joined the Coventry Enterprise Agency as its director for two years, helping the growth of self employment and small businesses in the city. After doubling the clientele and income of the agency, he returned to IBM as an agent manager drawing directly on his newly acquired experience of small firms.

IBM's director of personnel Len Peach joined the Health Service, initially as its director of personnel. Within a year he was promoted to chief executive. During his three year secondment, he helped improve the management systems and practices within the service. He has now returned to his former position with IBM.

A junior IBM personnel officer spent six months handling recruitment for Save the Children. The experience she gained meant she could return to a more responsible post at IBM.

A chief inspector from Chiswick police station undertook a three month study on work load for an IBM regional group. He returned to a post in Scotland Yard, where he is now concerned with the career development of police officers.

Case study: *Marks and Spencer*

Janet Walton and Gill Henderson from Marks and Spencer in Leicester took on an assignment through ARC's Compass scheme, a pilot project that ran for a year using assignments for development of management staff.

They spent 50 hours each on a part-time basis at Sofa, a community project recycling second-hand furniture to people on low incomes. After a period of research they were able to recommend ways of increasing donations and putting together mailing lists to target publicity. They also ran training sessions in customer care for staff and volunteers.

The results – increased income and greater awareness of Sofa in the surrounding area.

As for the two secondees, they were able to test new skills such as team working, planning, information analysis and general communication and negotiations skills. The assignment also gave them a broader social awareness and extended their outlook as well as their skills.

Case study: *Nationwide Anglia*

Nationwide Anglia was one of the first to pilot short term secondments to develop and challenge management trainees. The building society wanted to practise secondment but did not want to lose staff for long periods of time. ARC and Nationwide Anglia developed short 100 hour secondments with a specific project. Secondees are usually released for one day a week for a couple of months.

According to the Jack Rutley, the building society's head of management development, the scheme was feasible because it released staff for one or two days at a time. It helped a number of voluntary organizations and lifted the society's profile in the community while it widened the horizons of some of the employees.

ARC identified six projects in the London area and worked out with the organizations what skills were needed by the secondees who were to complete the projects. ARC matched seven mangement trainees with the projects on an induction day. The company also set up pilot projects that weren't restricted to management trainees in Northamptonshire, where the society has a large administrative base.

Two trainees did a survey on the effectiveness of Hampden Community Centre, London. The trainee managers drew up a questionaire which they sent to over 2,500 homes. The response was so low that they spent much of their secondment going to interview local residents on foot. During the survey they spoke to over 2,200 people including a high proportion of Bengali speakers and residents of a large council estate. Both felt the project had been very successful. They identified over 40 new facilities that people wanted and managed to find over 25 people who said they were willing to help out at the centre. The project increased the trainees' self confidence because they felt that they had managed it from beginning to end. One of the trainees also stated that the data handling techniques he had learned could be used to fine tune marketing for individual branches and increase sales turnover.

Rutley told the magazine, *Personnel Management* in January 1990: 'These projects called for a different approach to working within the secure confines of the Nationwide Building Society. Trainees have to demonstrate initiative, creativity and a fair amount of planning, and they they have to go out and execute their plan.'

Sam Walker was seconded to Choice, an advisory centre for disabled people. The two research workers from Choice needed guidance on recruitment of extra employees and some general advice. Walker provided them with a checklist to use while they were interviewing and left them with their own tailor-made personnel manual. Walker used his personnel department and ACAS to help. He also says that this practical experience of background personnel work will stand him in good stead when managing staff.

Case study: *Barclays Bank*

At any one time, between 70 and 80 Barclays' staff are in the community giving financial, management and administrative expertise to charities and enterprise agencies. Mid career 'return ticket' secondments give secondees a wider outlook, which should help their career development. They are normally attached to business initiatives such as Enterprise Agencies and the The Prince's Youth Business Trust. Staff give start up business advice and guidance. Pre-retirement secondees go to charities and often enjoy the experience so much that they carry on after they have retired. The bank pays for up to three years secondment, which can act as a bridge between work and retirement.

Small companies often can't spare the manpower for community work, but they can make employees aware of the possibilties available. Some companies list appeals for volunteers in their employee newsletter or magazines, others pin them to the company noticeboard.

Companies can also make their employees aware that almost everybody has something to offer in the way of an ability that a charity can make use of. It is helpful to appoint someone in the company, who is responsible for finding out what skills community groups require and for ensuring that employees hear about the openings. The appointee can arrange for charities to send representatives to talk to the employees about their work.

Lending people is clearly a lot more trouble than giving money, but the payoffs are potentially much higher.

6.3 Sponsorship

Sponsorship is a popular way of giving, while increasing market awareness and enhancing the image of a company. It differs from simple giving in that the commercial pay-off for the company is much more closely defined. Indeed, the best sponsorships are seen as partnerships between the company and the benefitting charity. Sponsorship also tends to be related to specific projects, rather than on-going support for established charities. Richard Busby from the company, Strategic Sponsorship, explains: 'Shell recently benefitted substantially from its past sponsorship record. As the judge implied very strongly in a very recent environmental court case, he would have fined Shell far more than the one million pounds imposed, but for their record in both environmental and community sponsorship.'

Case study: *British Telecom*

A senior executive BT admitted recently: 'We're in danger of being seen as bureaucratic, faceless, and sometimes apparently uncaring. I hope to see that image dead and buried. Our sponsorship budget may be small compared to our annual promotional spend, but we are now one of the largest corporate sponsors of the Arts and environmental projects in the UK. It's a fine balance between philanthropy and enlightened self interest, but we are looking for recognition for our not inconsiderable efforts.'

From a standing start two years ago, BT now puts £1 million a year into the medium across three areas, the Arts, the environment and the disabled. These range from travelling exhibitions to high profile involvement with the Royal Philharmonic Orchestra and the Royal Shakespeare Company. BT wants to be seen as improving the quality of life in the community and, unlike many sponsors, does not treat its programme as an additional tool in promoting product sales. Recently it has undertaken sponsorship of British Telecom New Contemporaries, a national tour of the best young UK artists.

Finance and insurance companies, building societies, banks and supermarkets all suffer similiar marketing problems. Consumers make decisions not on investment returns, but on factors such as empathy, confidence and recognition of brand names. Sponsorship is claimed to be more effective than advertising on all three counts.

However, a sponsorship programme cannot make a company something it is not. A food company may look to sponsor a sports event to give it a healthy image, but if doubts are cast about the validity of the product's health claims or associations, neither the sponsor nor the charity will benefit. If the sponsorship has to be withdrawn (for example, the British Heart Foundation will not renew its sponsorship with Van de Bergh, the makers of Flora margarine, a policy that it plans to extend to all food sponsors), the resultant bad publicity can be even worse for the sponsor.

According to Busby, there are eight main reasons why companies should consider sponsorship:

1. Increased awareness. The public is made generally aware that the company exists.
2. Corporate hospitality. This is the traditional form of sponsorship. Though still important, it is now heading down the list of priorities.
3. Image enhancement. Increasingly companies use sponsorship as part of a bigger overall campaign.
4. Attitudinal re-inforcement or shift. For instance, when a company wants to emphasize its stability and size, it may sponsor traditional upmarket activities such as cricket and opera.
5. Direct acquisition of new customers – if the firm has a stand where the event is being held.
6. Staff relations and recruitment. To enhance the company's image to would-be employees. Dull companies can seem exciting if they are associated with glamorous sports.
7. Investor and government relations. Istel, the Information and Technology Services Company, bought up this summer by AT&T, was previously contemplating a flotation and therefore sponsored the first ever outdoor performance of the Royal Opera at Kenwood last summer to attract the attention of opinion formers.

The opportunities for sponsorship are wide. Companies will normally select events to sponsor according to the following factors:
• cost: often negligible if the company simply guarantees any shortfall in income from an event, but equally can be very high (Blue Arrow's support for the British attempt on the America's Cup involved several millions and may have been an element in investor concern at how the company was managed)
• location: many companies prefer to focus on local events, where they can achieve greatest promotional impact
• the size and nature of the audience: how many of the target market will watch the event, or read the account in the press?
• prestige: is this an event that will enhance our reputation by

association? (not many companies openly sponsor fox hunting, for example)

● potential: will this activity grow in importance? Minority sports can grow to become prime time television events (e.g. snooker was a forgotten activity 15 years ago); companies that provide support in the early years can benefit substantially as the sport takes off.

● need: how important will our involvement be to this event or organization? There are often more benefits to a company from being the sole sponsor than from being just one of many.

Sponsorship tends to fall by volume into three categories:
– The Arts
– sport
– others.

6.3.1 *The Arts*

Even small companies can sponsor the Arts in a variety of ways. They can sponsor the exhibition of a local artist or a fashion show by local art college students. Or they can buy the work of local artists or sculptors to brighten up public areas of their premises – and perhaps to realise a profit. This would not only help the artist, but it could have unexpected benefits in years to come if they accumulate in value.

Large corporate sponsors often sponsor travelling exhibitions, which are more likely to reach a wider audience. Or they sponsor high profile events such as operas and ballets, hoping this will enhance their perception by the general public as a quality business.

Case study: *Barclays Bank*

As a founder member of the Association for Business Sponsorship of the Arts (ABSA), Barclays has been involved with Arts sponsorship since the mid 1970s. Says Brian Carr, head of Barclays Community Enterprise: 'We aim to ensure that the activities we sponsor are spread around the country as much as possible. We give help through regional offices for local events, which range from the Kings Lynn festival and Guildford Choral Society to the Cornwall male Voice Choir and Birmingham School of Music.'

Support on a national basis includes sponsorship of London City Ballet's 10th anniversary year, combining a new production of Swan Lake with a 40-venue regional tour and the Royal Ballet's visit to Australia as part of that country's bicentenary celebrations. Such sponsorships ensure that the Arts travel outside London and carry the name of Barclays with them.

Other sponsorships include the Barclays Young Painter Award, an annual prize of £10,000 for the most promising post graduate art student.

Barclays has also given £150,000 to the young National Trust Theatre, which puts on plays in National Trust venues. The touring project ensures that the bank gets maximum publicity value for its money.

Case study: *IBM*

IBM sponsors the Arts as part of its social responsibility programme, as a means of contributing to the quality of life in the community. The recent Leonardo Da Vinci Exhibition is among the initiatives it has sponsored. The exhibition, which opened in early 1989 at London's Hayward Gallery, was visited by 262,000 people and received great critical acclaim. It won the Association for Business Sponsorship of the Arts, Daily Telegraph Award for the best single Arts project of the year. Other recent Arts sponsorships include the opera house to be built in the grounds of Compton Verney, a stately home in Warwickshire. IBM produced a video to promote the project and held a concert to attract donations from Midlands industry and commerce, as well as making its own cash donation. It has also recently supported the commisioning of new works to mark the 25th anniversary of the Nash Ensemble and sponsored a production of Opera 80s Marriage of Figaro.

Case study: *British Rail*

British Rail is a patron of the Association of Business Sponsorship of the Arts. In 1986 it won the Business Sponsorship Incentive Scheme Industry Year Award for its scuplture commission at Brixton Station, South London. The three bronze statues of local people, by artist Kevin Atherton, stand on the station platform.

Other projects include a mural, for the platform waiting shelter at Frinton on Sea, Essex. The painting was created by members of the Frinton and Walton Heritage Trust and installed by a YTS team, sponsored by NACRO.

British Rail believes art contributes distinction and visual enrichment to an environment. It states in its brochure 'British Rail in the Community' that art can bring colour and vitality and is a tangible expression of quality and care and that 'it is our policy to encourage art and craftworks of integrity and imagination.'

Case study: *Thorn-EMI plc.*

Music represents a substantial part of Thorn EMI's commercial activities, so it is natural that it should favour sponsorship of musical events. The

1988/89 annual report encloses a booklet 'Responsible Business' which outlines the group's community activities in the financial year. Among initiatives covered in the booklet is the 1988 world premiere of Beethoven's Tenth Symphony presented by the Royal Philharmonic Society.

Thorn-EMI also supports individual institutions such as the Royal Albert Hall and the Royal Opera House. In addition, it contributed to the Jacqueline Du Pre Memorial Fund in 1989.

EMI Records gives substantial support to the Nordoff-Robins Music Therapy Centre in London, which uses music to rehabilitate handicapped children. EMI Records also sponsors classical music concerts.

Thorn-EMI gives financial subsidies to the Royal Academy of Arts and the National Theatre. It is also a member of the Association of Business Sponsorship of the Arts.

The company's policy on funding for the visual and performing arts allows it to give special consideration to events which promote contemporary works and encourage new artists.

6.3.2 *Sport*

Sponsoring televized sports such as football, horse jumping, golf or cricket reaches a wide audience and provides many additional opportunities to promote the company. But sponsoring small local events, such as a disabled sports day, can be equally effective in value for money terms.

Unusual or growing sports are also a lucrative area for sponsorship. Baseball, softball and Japanese wrestling are all increasing in popularity. Companies whose name is linked with them now, will reap the benefits if these sports follow the example of snooker or darts and become television events.

Case study: *B&Q*

B&Q uses football sponsorship as a means of cultivating strong community links. It has developed a unified, coherent approach to support a wide range of football-related activities. The company sponsored the Scottish Football League Championship in several ways. First, it produced the free-distribution B&Q League News Review. B&Q distributes 300,000 copies of the Review, which has grown from a four page pamphlet to a 12 page magazine, each season.

B&Q also targeted the under-fourteen section of the Scottish Schools Football Association. This opened a direct dialogue with the schools. The company followed this up by launching a nationwide Schools Cup Competition, which encouraged the 38 league clubs to allow the latter stages of the competition to be played on their grounds.

In addition the company works with the Scottish Football Association and its national and technical director to produce a Soccer Skills Poster to help provide a standard coaching base at all levels of the game in Scotland. The poster provided excellent publicity since it was distributed to schools, clubs and associations throughout Scotland. To back it up, B&Q organized coaching centres, where the best pupils from Scotland's schools competed against each other. The winners appeared at Hampden Park in August, prior to the Centenary Celebration Game.

B&Q also sponsored a Soccer Rules Poster designed to promote better knowledge of the rules of the game.

The DIY giant also sponsored the Scottish Womens Football Association team and arranged matches against England and Ireland.

A popular scheme that the company ran was a Panini Swap Shop for football stickers. B&Q held Panini Sticker Swapshops in its supercentres. Thousands of youngsters received free tickets for games as long as they brought an adult. On the day, a section of the ground was set aside for families and free crisps, soft drinks and goody bags were handed out courtesy of B&Q.

The blind have not been exempt from B&Q's good offices. B&Q's Football Today is printed by the Braille Press in Edinburgh and distributed nationally to blind fans.

The company has even used the football theme to integrate the mentally handicapped into the community, through free tickets to the Ark House Association for rehabilitating adults with a mental handicap. Staff organise travel to and from games and invite Ark House residents to accompany them to the B&Q League matches. B&Q has also extended the football sponsorship theme to raise money for other charities. This included donating money to Telethon for every goal scored in certain divisions of the football league as well as donating tickets, autographed footballs and other memorabilia to charitable causes. This has meant that store managers have become involved in many other charity schemes.

Case study: *British Telecom*

BT sponsors the Kielder Challenge, where teams of disabled and able bodied take part in outdoor events. The aim of the challenge is to promote teamwork, build self confidence and to open a challenging environment the youngsters would not normally encounter.

Thanks to BT support, the British Sports Association for the Disabled has enlarged its swimming championships and run a National Swimming Development programme. Among the skills the participants learnt were basic water safety techniques, which are vital if a disabled person is to enjoy water sports regularly.

There is no shortage of community orientated events such as sponsored walks, barn dances or hospital fetes, many of which are good opportunities to enhance your company's caring image.

It only takes a bit of imagination. Entrust one manager with the job of scouring the pages of the local paper to identify interesting sponsorship opportunities. Or phone up your local newspaper and ask for the names of people who are involved in charities in the area. After a talk with charity organisers you will have more ideas than you can deal with.

6.3.3 Community activities

Case study: *Asda Stores*

Asda wanted a corporate sponsorship to build a solid base with its local community and improve relationships with local authorities. After research, top management decided that the customer they needed to impress was a busy woman with children. And the company wanted to cement relationships with local authorities as it continued its expansion programme. So Asda became a summer holiday activity programme sponsor. The retail group provides the money and helps with information leaflets, T-shirts for helpers and hats for kids. Store managers took part in over 85% of the events, often dressed up as clowns. Local newspaper photographers were able to catch unusual and funny shots and Asda received widespread coverage.

Case study: *Rover Group*

Rover sponsors a school libraries programmme so that school leavers will be aware of the company name and will perhaps think of the company when they choose a career and an employer.

6.3.4 Sponsored research

Sponsored research has become an increasing proportion of the revenue of Britain's universities and polytechnics over the past decade. Company sponsorship of research extends from the technical to pure science, from social science to strategic management.

Although a high proportion of this activity is directly related to commercial benefit, much is also of more general benefit. Companies gain a reputation for involvement in innovation and special relationships with polytechnics and universities. Bright post-graduate students, for example, can be directed by their tutors towards the company for employment.

Case study: *BP*

The *Financial Times* bills BP's Venture Research as 'one of the world's most imaginative corporate research programmes'. For the past 10 years BP has funded speculative science in a wide field from advanced mathematics to biology. The research does not need to have any relation to BP's oil, energy and chemical businesses – or any foreseeable industrial application at all. The fund supports scientists who are researching ideas considered too unorthodox to be funded by corporate R&D departments or public agencies.

BP transferred its portfolio of research and intellectual property rights to Venture Research International in 1990. It has become a corporate shareholder alone with a number of major corporations, such as Sony, whose interests together span the industrial spectrum.

Among the projects sponsored is an investigation by two botanists on the three dimensional structure of the genetic material (chromosomes) in cells.

The research was important because, although thousands of scientists worldwide were unravelling the chemical sequence of DNA within chromosomes no-one had looked at the arrangement of chromosomes within the cell nucleus. The two botanists received £100,000 a year, which enabled them to develop new techniques for investigating the structure of cell nuclei and start to apply them to human genes.

While many of these 'pump-priming' activities have led to nothing, others have stimulated advances of substantial commercial value. One project, for example, subsequently received over £7 million of Government money, because it had great significance for the pharmaceutical industry.

Checklist
1. Does your company have someone responsible for identifying and evaluating sponsorship opportunities?
2. Does your company have a sponsorship policy? a sponsorship budget?
3. Does your company measure the benefits of sponsorship activities?

6.4 Education and schools liaison

Not so long ago, companies and schools used to have very little contact with each other. Awareness of difficulties facing employees in recruiting young people in the next few years, coupled with a push from government and elsewhere for more contact across the business and education divide has begun to change all that.

Companies can obtain substantial benefits from involvement with schools. For example, they have an opportunity to influence and improve the curricula. If schools have a clear idea what sort of skills are needed in the outside world, then the company needs to spend less money on remedial training for school leavers.

If a company has a high profile in local schools, the better recruits are more inclined to apply for a job there. For example, the Norwich Union, which has a head office in Norwich, needs a good slice of the town's school leavers, so it is important that it is well respected in the community. Other companies take the attitude that today's pupils are tomorrow's customers, so it is vital to influence both them and their parents in a positive fashion. The return on investment can be substantial. For example, the value of a young person who opens a bank account and then stays with that bank for his/her working lifetime is a minimum of £500,000.

Business in the Community is unequivocal about the positive advantages for all parties involved. It states in a booklet on education/business partnerships that a schools involvement policy will benefit:
Young people
– through better motivation, attainment and qualifications
– through greater self confidence and having more to offer to society
– through a greater understanding of what business, work and enterprise are all about
– through vocational training that is more closely linked to education in school and is relavant to available jobs
– through better chances of a worthwhile job, combined with training.
Schools and colleges will benefit from:
– a richer curriculum and greater capacity for developing it through wider contacts with industry
– improved mangement skills at a time when head teachers and principals are being given financial control of schools and colleges
– new resources for learning including local employers, workplace environments and materials
– access to equipment and other material resources.
Employers will gain from:
– a potentially better qualified and well motivated work force
– an opportunity to influence the curriculum of schools and colleges

– development of staff through contact with education and the community
– a range of services which schools and colleges can offer to improve the effectiveness of local employers
– a more stable and prosperous local environment in which to trade
– an opportunity to enhance their reputation in the local community.

BiC explains that even before these partnerships developed, businesses had been inviting children into their premises on work experience and participating in school life. The new schemes often only formalized existing arrangements.

Case study: *IBM*

IBM UK, the British subsidary of IBM, the world's largest computer company, gives just over £2 million a year to educational activities, one of its five select priorities. Its overall aim is to build educational partnerships with an emphasis on growing teachers' management skills, encouraging students to continue in higher education and helping them to prepare for working with information technology.

As part of the programme, IBM staff are allowed to spend up to 10% of their working time on approved community activities and they are actively encouraged to take on posts such as school governorships. The company's four main educational priorities are schools, education and training for 16–19 year olds, higher education and adult education. These four activities are plotted against five key IBM operational interests

- development of its market
- influencing the public policy debate
- recruiting and training
- investment in the community
- research.

For example, the company sees a link with a school not as a community investment but as a marketing strategy. The company does not like giving straight donations of computers to schools and educational institutions, although it does offer personal computing equipment plus software and support, often at 60% of retail price. Instead, it uses IBM's expertise to offer free management training to teachers. Two-day teacher management workshops for deputy heads and heads of departments are run at IBM locations around the UK and were attended in 1989 by more than 225 senior teachers representing 187 schools. One reason for the strong interest in these courses is the government thrust for schools to run themselves more as businesses.

IBM's manufacturing and development centres at Havant, Greenock and Hursley ran lectures for the Institute of Mechanical Engineers. Called the Leonardo Da Vinci Lectures, they were aimed at encouraging young people towards careers in information technology. More than 20,000 students attended the roadshow at 52 locations in the UK and Ireland.

In addition, the IBM Institute backs the use of information technology in teaching through projects with schools, polytechnics and colleges. IBM also backs training initiatives through a number of associations including the Foundation for Education Business Partnerships and Business in the Arts.

IBM Desk Top Publishing Systems have been donated to 19 university subject centres established in 1989 under a joint initiative of the Computer Board for Universities and Research Councils and the University Funding Committee.

The St Paul's Open Learning Technology centre in Bristol opened its doors in November 1989. Its aim is to help the unemployed in inner city areas find jobs by offering them free computer courses. IBM employees are helping out and the company has donated its machines.

6.4.1 *What kinds of involvement can companies take?*

Companies can increase the volume of school leaver applicants they receive by providing more opportunities for the number of local school children to receive short periods of work experience. However, these opportunities need to be planned and managed to give the young people an understanding of how rewarding work can be. All too many employers simply give them a routine, mundane job such as photocopying all day – and are subsequently surprised that the youngsters emerge with a negative view of working for that organization. Companies can also open their doors for open days, parents evenings, career talks and pupil visits, and use educational links to sponsor careers fairs, school teams, clubs, trips and award schemes. The community becomes positively aware of the company's presence in a positive fashion. These regular, co-ordinated links with schools can give a company a distinct competitive edge over rivals in the local employment market.

Companies can also get involved in the local community through government funded Compacts. There are over 50 of these formal partnerships between inner city schools and business. The Compacts are designed to meet local educational and recruitment needs and involve pupils, parents and employers. The original aims were to raise standards of performance and attendance at school, to encourage more young people to continue their education after 16; and to influence employers, especially those in the inner city areas to change their attitudes towards educational links. The first Compact, which was modelled on an original in Boston, Massachusetts, was run by the Inner London Education Authority and local employers including Whitbread.

Young people work with their school and parents towards a set of measurable personal goals and standards. These include academic progress and personal and social development. Schools and colleges commit themselves to work towards specific targets for their students as they progress through education and training to take their place in the workforce. Finally, the employer's part of the deal is to agree to give jobs with training or training leading to a job to the youngsters, who manage to achieve their targets. Firms can therefore recruit from well-motivated achievers.

If there are no Compacts in your area, you can always set up an 'education/business partnership' promoted by Business in the Community. Trade unions, voluntary groups, small employers, education officials and other interested parties are encouraged to set up a steering group, make a joint statement of policy and outline a programme of action with a time scale and performance review.

Companies can also get involved in the newly created Training and Enterprise Councils. These are designed to take over from the Training Agency which ran large national training programmes. The TECs will offer a more localized opportunity for education action. Senior managers of local companies sit on the board alongside academics and advisors. The TECs are financed mainly by government money but, according to James Jolly at Business in the Community, the government hopes that employer participation on TECs will encourage businesses, too, to invest in training youngsters in their communities.

Universities and polytechnics also offer endless possibilities to companies which are willing to exploit them. Larger companies like to sponsor either posts or courses at educational institutions. This is a good way of getting the company's name known in a particular area.

As grants decrease in real terms, more and more employers are realising the advantages of subsidising a student through college or university. With, for example, science and computer graduates in short supply and an expected eventual shortfall of graduates in all disciplines, this is a practical way of laying claim to high calibre graduate employees.

Another popular and less expensive method is to open your doors to undergraduates for work experience. The company can spot talent early and make an offer well before the student graduates.

Case study: *British Gas*

British Gas' educational policy covers almost the whole spectrum of education, from universities to primary schools. At a higher education level it funds academic posts, ranging from a British Gas lecturer in Energy and Buildings at Oxford Polytechnic through to a fellowship for women returners into science and engineering at the University of Surrey and research study into gerontology at the University of Birmingham.

It also sponsors Sci-Tech, an international scientific film and television festival held every two years in Bristol. Says Tony Wyatt, head of the social policy unity at British Gas, 'Bristol stages this festival partly to boost the city for visitors from the rest of Britain and abroad. We sponsor it partly as a demonstration of support for the Bristol community, partly to support this particular art form, partly to increase awareness of the importance of science and technology to all our lives, and partly to allow us the facility to contribute to extra curricular activities at universities by running a university roadshow of the winning entries.'

British Gas higher education sponsorships are limited to its own employees. It funds, among others, an annual MA in Business information at the University of Edinburgh, two scholarships a year at the Guildhall School of Music and Drama, support for mature female students at graduate and post graduate level at the Lucy Cavendish College, Cambridge, and six Scholarships at the University of Strathclyde every year for students from developing countries.

At the other end of the educational spectrum, the company is also backing research into how primary teachers' process scientific information and a doctoral thesis on children's understanding of energy-related software at the Institute of Education at London University.

Schools involvement
Wyatt explained at a conference on social responsibility that the company maintains a warehouse in West London where users can obtain free or heavily subsidized educational materials. The catalogue alone runs to 60 pages. Schools and the general public can also use the company's film and video library. All publications are drawn up along guidelines suggested by the National Consumer Council's 'Guidelines for business sponsors of educational material'. Many of the materials are designed by teachers for

teachers and evaluation is invited by those who use them, and by Her Majesty's Inspectors.

Schools and teachers need much more than materials. So British Gas sends out over 200 staff to visit schools regularly and give presentations on a range of energy-related topics. A 'Science of the Flame' lecture is popular with 12 to 14 year olds, for example.

In addition, staff in the regions hire out gas cookers so that pupils can gain practical experience on modern appliances. The company also supports two theatre companies 'Molecule' and 'Floating Point' that use drama to show the young how exciting maths and science can be. Other exciting activities have included a Treasure Trail competition for schools to back up the sponsorship of the National Heritage Memorial Fund's exhibition 'Treasures for the Nation' at the British Museum.

Recently, British Gas has helped develop the new national curriculum and supported the design and technology work at the University of Salford and through the National Business and Information Studies Centre. It also funds Leeds University's Learning in Science Project, which explores how young people can be challenged and motivated to take a greater interest in science and technology, and a bus to tour girls schools for the Women into Science and Engineering campaign (WISE). The vehicle is equipped with work stations with microelectronics, pneumatics, computer-aided design.

Nonetheless, British Gas has taken a cautious attitude towards government initiatives in education and schools liaison. Says Wyatt: 'The considerable ramifications of our liaison service and the extensive other linkages that we have developed have tended to make us cautious in recent times in embracing the numerous voluntary and government initiatives, with which we have all been faced over the last 10 or 15 years. Whilst we are strong supporters of Business in the Community we have not been in the van of developing education-business partnerships, at least not in the sense of 'local' partnerships. My company is so far only involved in a handful of Compacts and only three TEC's and we shall want to see how universally they develop before we adapt our traditional links dramatically.'

'In the meantime, our intention is to develop mutual experience. On the one hand, to encourage more of our employees to become more involved with the work of the schools by becoming school governors, for example. And on the other, by encouraging more of the school population, undergraduates and teachers to come into our company to experience for themselves the world of industry and commerce. In this respect, we are developing arrangements with the organization 'Understanding British Industry' to give senior teachers the opportunity of benefitting from our Management Development and Training programme.'

Other organizations the company has supported include the Association for Science Education, the National Association of Environmental Education and the Centre for the Study of Comprehensive Schools, and Education 2000, a teaching experiment based in Milton Keynes, which investigates modern technology teaching and methods.

6.4.2 How to organise educational activities

Business in the Community (BiC) in its booklet 'Writing a boardroom policy' outlines the importance of a written company document for companies that want a co-ordinated, effective educational policy. It emphasizes that written guidelines ensure support is concentrated on those educational activities which have been identified as beneficial to the company. They give justification to the expenditure of management time and resources by identifying clear commercial benefits to the company.

The booklet states that in a recent survey involving managers from Marks and Spencers and Royal Mail Parcels the most commonly expressed incentive to take action was the publication of a policy statement endorsed by the board. However, this may still not be enough and BiC suggests other ways to encourage action.

• include educational responsibility in appropriate job descriptions
• set job targets and include in annual appraisals
• give the local manager a small budget to spend on school links activities
• give personal recognition from the chief executive or senior manager
• nominate a person in each location to be expert on the various government initiatives and on what other independent link bodies can contribute and who can co-ordinate the company's local activities.

Checklist
A) Schools liaison
1. Do you have difficulties in recruiting school leavers?
2. Do your local managers have a budget for educational activities? Are they assessed on their achievements in this field?
3. Do you offer access to your company through work experience and/or pupil visits?
4. Do you have a planned strategy for involvement in local educational activities?

5. Have you developed a close partnership with at least one local school?
6. Do you have a system for identifying any surplus material you could give to schools?
7. Could you fund any prizes for achievement on certain parts of the curriculum?
8. Do you encourage employees to become school governors?
9. Could your company provide any of the following to local schools?
   - career talks and counselling
   - explanatory leaflets and videos
   - holiday jobs
   - interview training
   - joint work projects
   - teacher secondment
   - inclusion of teachers on company training courses

B) University liaison
1. Could you fund a university post?
2. Could you fund any courses?
3. Could you subsidize a student through a degree course?
4. Could you sponsor a university road show or careers fair?

6.5 Small business development

Businesses cannot live in isolation from the broader community any more than they can live in isolation from their markets. They rely on those communities for staff and customers as well as shareholders and the support of opinion leaders. The belief that a company's community contribution was to run an efficient, profitable company has become increasingly untenable. For many companies, the watershed came in July 1981 with the Toxteth and Brixton riots. Part of the solution, according to Michael Heseltine, then Environment Secretary, was business involvement in the community, through enlightened self interest.

In response to this, Business in the Community (BiC) was formed as an umbrella organization to bring the voluntary sector, trade unions and local and central government together. To date it has over 300 members. Enterprise Agencies are the building blocks of the organization. There were only 28 when the organization was formed in 1982; now there are over 314.

But what are enterprise agencies and what do they do?

These organizations are operated as limited companies. They

offer help and advice to people running small businesses as well as those hoping to start one up. Many run for their clients small business clubs, which meet regularly to swap experiences and learn about new management techniques or regulations. The agencies often organize training courses or 'meet the buyer' sessions to introduce small businesses to potential big customers.

Money comes from the government, but is dependent on equal or greater sums from the private sector. A host of companies regularly second highly qualified people to help run enterprise agencies across England and Wales.

There were, of course, a number of enterprise agencies, even before the formation of BiC. For example, in 1979, Lenta (the London Enterprise Agency) was created because a group of major companies felt that they should play a significant role in tackling inner city dereliction in London. According to Lenta's 1989 annual report, they also wished to encourage other companies to follow suit in other cities. This role was later passed onto BiC after it was created in 1981. Since 1979, Lenta has provided business counselling to over 50,000 people and provided entrepreneurial training to over 14,000.

BAT Industries helped launch the Southampton Enterprise Agency in 1981 with a guarantee of full funding for the first two years. This enabled a supporters club to be developed in parallel, whose members eventually became contributors to expenses. BAT continued its support with secondees from its member companies, while National Westminster and Barclays provided one secondee each on a two year basis from 1983. In its first five years the agency handled over 5,000 inquiries and conducted over 2000 counselling sessions, leading to almost 600 business start ups or expansions. During this time there were only 24 known failures – a rate of only four per cent.

Case study: *Royal Dutch/Shell Group of Companies*

Shell is one of the leaders in the field, setting up first a small business unit and now operating its community activities through the Shell Enterprise Unit. As a founder member of LENTA, the London Enterprise Agency, Shell has regularly seconded staff to the organization. Experience taught the company that there were several key areas where it could be most effective. These included running training courses for would-be entrepreneurs, providing counselling and advice and developing small industrial and commercial units for embryo businesses.

In the mid eighties the company wholly funded several ventures of this kind. Two examples are the Broad Oak Enterprise Village at Sittingbourne, Kent and Carrington Business park near Manchester. At Sittingbourne, Shell paid for the £400,000 conversion of its laboratories into an enterprise village. It undertook a similar scheme in a redundant cluster of buildings on 17 acres within the 300 acre Shell Chemicals Carrington plant. Over 50 companies established themselves at Carrington in the first phase of the project. As other companies became interested in the area, they brought with them new jobs and prospects for the locals.

BiC draws together a host of other initiatives promoting business involvement in the community. These include Young Enterprise, a national charity that gives young people the chance to run a scaled down version of a company, through to Project Fullemploy, which brings together public and private bodies dedicated to helping young people of mainly ethnic origin fulfil their potential through training. Shell has guaranteed funds until 1991 for one of these initiatives, Livewire, an organization formed to help 18–25 year olds create their own work.

Case study: *Barclays Bank*

Barclays has worked hard to help people hit hard by unemployment. Back in 1989 the government closed the Sunderland shipyard. More than 6000 people were forced onto the dole. Brian Carr, head of Barclays Community Enterprise at Fleetway House, London, acted quickly: 'We have always been a strong bank in Sunderland, so after a few phone calls and arm twisting in certain quarters we put together a loan fund with soft capital repayment to help the redundant start up small businesses on their own.'

By the end of 1989, 12 small businesses had taken advantage of the scheme. Brian said: 'People set up businesses in design and manufacture of furnishings and desk top publishing. When you are loaning to small operations you have to make sure that you are giving to organizations that can operate successfully without buying expensive equipment.'

Over the last two years Barclays has given over £400,000 to establish loan funds to help set up small companies in areas such as Cleveland, Newcastle, Manchester, Greater London and Devon and Cornwall.

Carr also seized the chance to use some of the experience he gained as deputy of the bank's agricultural team for 10 years.

'Northumberland was suffering a serious decline in the agricultural and mining industries. I realised that tourism could take up some of the slack. So I set up a Tourism Development Project to encourage people to take holidays in the area, which has a rich Roman and Christian heritage. We aimed to educate the farmers and small shop keepers to provide a better service, so we set up an award scheme, which has successfully made these small concerns aware of tourists' needs.'

Companies can also make a significant contribution to the establishment and growth of small businesses by making specialist expertise available, either through development/enterprise agencies or schemes set up by professional bodies. For example, the Teeside branch of the Chartered Institute of Marketing recently set up a Marketing Advice Centre, and aimed at helping small businesses apply effective marketing to their activities.

7 Responsibilities towards the environment

'The environment will be one of the most important political issues of the 1990's, notwithstanding events in Eastern Europe', claims the CBI in a report on a survey conducted jointly with the leading international management and technology consultancy, PA Consulting Group.

Entitled 'Waking up to a better environment', the report goes on to state that one of the key areas for debate will be the tensions between pressures for a tougher regulatory regime and the need to allow corporate social responsibility and market pressure to generate environmentally beneficial policies.

Part of the problem will be defining exactly where companies' environmental responsibilties begin and end. Certainly any organization that assumes it will have a good environmental record simply by not emitting any dangerous or noxious waste products from manufacture is living in a fool's paradise. Increasingly, a company's environmental performance is also measured by how proactive it is in areas such as:
- reducing noise pollution
- demanding that its suppliers do not use environmentally harmful products
- energy efficiency
- active participation in improving the environment, for example through inner city development
- encouragement of environmental initiatives.

As the *Financial Times* expresses it (21 June 1990): 'Saatchi's research shows that people now expect companies to be environmentally aware in every area of their activities. Companies cannot expect people to be impressed by their new green product or by their advertisement – if they do not take a responsible attitude to the environment in areas such as corporate strategy or production planning.'

The CBI report points out that penalties for non-compliance will increase at the same time: 'A shift towards polluter-pays taxation, ultimately to be manifested through a carbon tax, for example, will be matched by a growth in environmentally-based litigation. The lessons of the Exxon Valdez oil spill have spread further than the problems of the clean-up operation.'

Already many companies are setting themselves tough environmental guidelines in the belief that self regulation is preferable to imposed government regulation.

These companies have found that good environmental management is also an investment. It can
- improve the company's reputation
- boost employee morale
- help attract high calibre recruits
- increase efficiency and cut costs by eliminating avoidable waste
- improve profits, by turning waste into marketable by-products.

The report maintains that failing to adopt environmentally responsible policies and behaviour can lead to:
- fines
- higher costs
- lost profits
- a sullied reputation
- as well as the possibility of stricter legislation and higher penalties.

Among possible future devlopments on the environmental issue, the authors of 'Waking up to a better environment' predict: 'Insurance companies will be more thorough in their investigation before issuing cover. Other institutional investors will be more vigilant before subscribing funds. Customers and suppliers will seek evidence of a compatible code of conduct'. Research has already identified a number of companies which are scrutinizing their suppliers 'green' record with a view to ceasing business with those who do not meet specifications of environmental responsibility. The evidence suggest that investors, too, are becoming more conscious of environmental risk.

7.1 Pollution control

What are the key issues on a socially responsible company's 'green' agenda? The CBI/PA survey discovered that companies perceived air pollution to be a high priority. The disposal of solid waste and effluent also featured as major issues for concern. So we start with these issues, all of which belong under the general heading of pollution prevention.

Case study: *3M*

3M, a diversified manufacturing company which employs 83000 people in 52 countries, was one of the first to implement an environmental programme. The UK subsidary, which employs over 5000 people at over 20 locations, started the successful Pollution Prevention Pays (3P) in 1977.

Up to 1988, the UK programme had saved the company over £6,831,900 with 86 projects. It has reduced air emmisions by 4,711 tonnes annually, solid waste by 1,878 tonnes per year and water effluent by 34.3 gallons per year. The savings are always calculated in the first year of the projects so the real figures are a lot higher than this. Worldwide, it is calculated that the environmental policy has saved the company over $420 million.

Explains Dr Richard Smith, environment, safety and security manager: 'In 1975 we realised it was to our advantage to look at waste minimisation technology. We decided to improve existing processes.'

In addition to 3M's global environmental policy, the UK company has its own vision and strategy. This includes a six point programme:

● to develop closer working relationships between its manufacturing, engineering, research and development, technical and marketing employees on environmental issues

● to develop less environmentally harmful products and processes that meet or anticipate the needs of the marketplace

● to develop internal awareness of 3M's environmental policies and build environmental responsibility into all aspects of 3M's UK operations

● to develop links with relevant governmental, industrial, professional, community and education groups, keeping them informed of 3M's environmental interests

● to work with suppliers and contractors to ensure that they provide products and services that do not transmit environmental problems to 3M or its customers

● to encourage and support employee initiatives that contribute to an improved environment at work, at home and in the local community.

The company has published a booklet called 'Environmental Ethics', which outlines its activities in this field. Written by freelance journalists it aims to educate employees, shareholders and customers on evironmental issues and its environmental policy in particular. The pamphlet states why the company is becoming increasingly concerned with the 'green' issue:

'The environmentally-concerned consumer is not just the individual who shops at supermarkets or in the High Street. It may also be a company, a distributor, even a major customer. Already many 3M customers are asking for goods that do not produce by-products and wastes and for evidence of 3M's commitment to producing "environment-friendly" goods.

'Significantly, during 3M recent corporate image research carried out among business audiences in four European countries – Spain, Sweden, West Germany and The Netherlands – one in five of all respondents said that "concern for the environment" was the most important attribute they would look for in a prospective supplier. By comparison, "value for money" was ranked the key attribute by 17 per cent of respondents.'

3M has a directive that 25% of capital must be generated from products less than five years old. This means that 3M invests heavily in R & D – it has spent over $2.8 billion in the past five years. By taking the opportunity to minimize pollution during development, it can bring products to market with minimal environmental effects.

An expanded environmental programme, 3P Plus, was introduced in 1988. In June 1989 the Operations Committee in St Paul, the company's US headquarters, raised the corporate target, to aim at reducing worldwide emissions by 90% by the year 2000.

Checklist
1. Does your company have an environmental policy encompassing a wide range of issues?
2. Does it have a system to monitor each of these issues and alert it to new issues?
3. Is someone responsible for monitoring performance and reporting to the board and to shareholders?

7.1.1 *Water pollution*

The government is about to bring in stringent new environmental guidelines on water pollution. Self regulation with the help of experts in the industry is better than imposed regulation. The water industry is at present engaged in a massive investment programme to improve the quality of Britains bathing beaches. The oil industry too continues to invest considerable sums in marine research, helping to improve our knowledge base and so define appropriate environmental control strategies for the North Sea in particular.

However all companies should be examining their effluent emissions. It not only makes economic sense to minimise this waste, it shows environmental acumen too.

What can you do? Among obvious steps:

- Any pollution programme must have the support of the board to succeed. This support should be enshrined in an environmental policy statement with specific reference to water pollution.
- Companies should maintain close contact with their water authority, which will be glad to give advice. Ideally, an organization should ensure that it has regular contact with a relevant specialist at the authority. Frank discussions with a person you can trust can help resolve problems at an early stage.
- Make sure your company is monitoring effluent emissions and is up to date on current anti-pollution technology in your field.
- Ensure that the relevant staff are familiar with the nature of your discharge. Ensure that they are committed to any pollution prevention programme by informing them of its importance through training sessions, booklets and the company newsletter.
- Either employ a water pollution specialist, environmental expert or assign the responsibility to an existing member of staff. Part of his or her task will be to keep up with current and proposed legislation and ensure that the company remains well within prescribed discharge limits. To be caught unawares, if stringent new regulations are enacted, could mean costly expenditure on new equipment, at short notice and at worst, large fines.

Case study: *ICI and the North Sea*

ICI is planning a multi-million pound investment to completely eliminate, by the mid 1990s, the disposal in the North Sea of chemical waste arising from its methyl methacrylate (MMA) manufacturing operations at Billingham on Teeside. MMA is a key raw material, which is used to supply ICI's growing business in acrylic polymers, which in turn form the basis for products such as 'Perspex' sheet for baths and shop signs.

Most of the expenditure will be on a sulphuric acid recovery plant to process the large volume of acidic ammonium sulphate effluent from the MMA operation. At the moment, this is shipped out and dumped in the North Sea under licence from the Ministry of Agriculture and Food.

Although extensive research over the past 10 years by both government and ICI scientists continues to indicate that sea disposal does not significantly harm marine life, ICI has decided to stop its river and sea programme entirely, on the grounds that public concern is an important consideration in its own right.

The decision has been taken within ICI's overall corporate commitment to improving the environmental performance of its plants. The new investment will secure the existing MMA operation at Billingham for the foreseeable future.

Case study: *ICI, Teeside*

'Over the centuries, the Tees estaury has been a focal point for tens of thousands of migrating birds. In more recent times, it has become a Mecca for a number of international industries and the birthplace of ICI, one of the world's leading chemical companies. The river itself became a victim of industrial success and was becoming one of the most polluted stretches in the world by the 1960s,' says David Bellamy in a booklet 'The Tees: The Living River'.

Now ICI and all the large companies, which use the river, are cleaning up their act. ICI has assigned laboratory facilities to monitor effluents and staff to investigate ways of reducing pollution.

Discharges have been reduced fourfold so far. This is reflected in an increase of species found by ICI's Brixham laboratory, from 33 to 81 since 1978. ICI has achieved the reduction in effluent discharge by measures such as installing a new £6 million ammonium sulphate plant, which converts waste into low grade fertilizer.

Case study: *J. Sainsbury*

Sainsbury's new 'Greencare' range of household cleaning products has been formulated with the environment in mind. The seven products are free from additives that cause pollution and are formulated whenever possible from vegetable-based ingredients that are renewable and bio-degradable. None of the products have been tested on animals.

Sainsbury's was the first UK supermarket to stock products from Ecover, the company that specializes in environmentally friendly cleaning products.

Case study: *HP Bulmer Holdings*

Cidermakers Bulmers won the 1983 Pollution Abatement Technology Award by developing a new method of dealing with its pectin effluent.

Bulmer is one of the world's major pectin producers. However, untreated waste from a plant that gets its pectin from citrus fruit is highly polluting and costly to treat in a conventional sewage works.

The Bulmer research team developed a bacterial culture that reduced the troublesome organic content of the pectin residues. This enabled the Welsh Water Authority to charge the plant less for waste water processing. Bulmer's new treatment plant cost £24,000 to install, but its cost savings on effluent treatment are estimated to be over £30,000 per year. The company believes there is yet further scope for improvement.

Case study: *The Distillers Company*

The Distillers Company won one of the first Angling Foundation Gold Medal Nationwide Awards for cleaning up discharges from 20 of its whisky distilleries in Scotland.

Distillery effluents are not directly poisonous, but they reduce the amount of oxygen in the river. Fish die if a river does not have enough oxygen. Instead of dumping the effluent straight in the river, Distillers now uses the protein recovered from the waste to make more than 200,000 tonnes of animal feed. Half of this food is sold abroad, so Distillers is cleaning up its act and making a valuable contribution to the UK balance of payments.

Checklist
1. Does your company monitor its fluid wastes, if any?
2. Are they at the minimum possible level, within current technology?

7.1.2 *Air pollution*

Wise manufacturing companies, recognizing the trend towards tighter and tighter air pollution controls at both national and supranational levels, are taking early preventive action.

Precedent has already been set by the CFC issue, which highlighted the importance of monitoring and controlling dangerous atmospheric emissions. Some companies predicted the problems ahead and acted quickly to get rid of CFCs in their manufacturing process. These later had the advantage of being able to claim that they had been in the vanguard of any environmental movement. Moreover, as public interest and media attention in the issue increased and the government started to look at the problem, these companies did not lose sales and could claim to be greener than slower-moving competitors.

So what can concerned organizations do to improve their clean air image? The CBI suggests that companies should:
• monitor and audit air emissions. This can help improve profit margins and will provide factual data to tackle complaints
• keep abreast of changing technologies. Timing change for the most opportune time can save costs and avoid unnecessary disruption of production
• look out for environmental pressure and legislative change. Early signals can help influence decisions or help you prepare for the change

- record all wastes, the improvements achieved and the responsibilities of company personnel.

However, companies have to make sure that they get their research right. After all, it would defeat the object, if a company introduced an alternative chemical which was later found also to be environmentally unsound.

Companies that don't cause atmospheric pollutants directly can still benefit from an environmental audit that focuses on these areas. They can, for example, ensure that the products they buy or stock are themselves produced by environmentally friendly processes. They can also ensure that the polystyrene cups they buy for coffee machines are not made with processes that use CFCs. They can also keep abreast of new developments on the use of 'greenhouse gases' in fire extinguishers and other products.

Case study: *3M*

Central to 3M's latest comprehensive pollution programme, 3P Plus, introduced in 1988, is a £150 million investment in air pollution control equipment to reduce the company's annual worldwide solvent emissions by more than 55,000 tonnes.

Dr Richard Smith, environmental, safety and security manager, says: 'There are four key points to emphasize. Firstly, the effort is entirely voluntary. Secondly, the reductions are beyond any necessary to ensure regulatory compliance. Thirdly, there is little or no economic benefit to 3M; and fourthly, it reflects 3M's commitment to improving the environment.'

Part of the plan includes installation of additional control equipment at all facilities that are major sources of hydrocarbons, even if the facilities are in areas that already meet government air quality standards. 3M's UK plants at Atherstone and Gorseinon are included in this phase of the programme.

Out of the total 3P Plus investment of £150 million, most will be spent in the US. The US has 95 3M plants in 40 states, many of them built in the early twentieth century.

3M plans to spend £30 million outside the US to reduce air emissions by more than 10,000 tonnes a year. This will result in the elimination or control of some 80% of 3M's air emissions. The 3M facilities involved have a deadline of 1993 to install the necessary air emission control equipment.

Since 1974, however, 3M has set out to develop new technology which aims to eliminate pollution at source. For example, traditional methods of making adhesive paper used chemical solvents, which emitted toxic substances into the atmosphere as they passed through the drying chamber. Now 3M has developed a water-based solvent for the coating process. The Atherstone factory has applied the new solvents to manufacture of abrasive paper, with substantial reductions in air pollution.

Another relevant new technology is a hot melt process, used at Atherstone since 1987 to apply adhesive to abrasive discs. This replaced the traditional process where adhesive was applied from a solution containing a volatile, non-toxic hydrocarbon solvent. This could not be recovered because of the large air dilution of the exhaust system and eventually escaped into the atmosphere.

3M now saves over £150,000 a year from it, while reducing the amount of solvent released into the atmosphere by over 75 tonnes.

Case study: *Linpac Plastics International*

Linpac Plastics International, one of Europe's biggest producers of expanded polystyrene, had been entirely dependent on CFCs until late 1988. According to Industrial Society magazine in December 1989, it cost Linpac a six figure sum, a total rearrangement of 30,000 square feet of factory space and the re-training of 360 staff to stop using the ozone depletant.

The move followed intergovernmental discussions in early 1987. These proposed a 50% reduction by 1997 of CFC 11/12, which Linpac used as a blowing agent for trays and boxes, and an eventual total ban on the substances.

Although packaging companies which used CFCs as a blowing agent only took up 2% of the world's CFC use, this 2% is still important. Linpac literature states: 'If the packaging industry ... uses CFCs of any grade, it is most definitely contributing to ozone depletion and the greenhouse effect.'

Some companies replaced CFCs with HCFC materials, which are similar to CFCs, but have much lower ozone depletion potential. Linpac felt this was not enough. Managing director Peter O'Shea and his researchers looked at alternative blowing agents and settled on pentane, a hydrocarbon that the company had stopped using in 1987. Pentane was chosen because it did not harm the ozone layer, is not a greenhouse gas and breaks down rapidly at low atmospheric levels. Pentane is a low level pollutant, but according to Linpac 'the environmental impact of expanded polystyrene production is regarded by experts as infinitesimally small compared to other sources such as emissions from motor vehicles. The switch to pentane had no significant impact on product performance.'

By March 1989 – way ahead of any international directives and before most companies had even thought about changing their processes to tackle the problem, Linpac was able to stamp its meat trays, fast food boxes and egg boxes with the slogan 'CFC FREE'.

Case study: *Friends of the Earth*

Friends of the Earth (FOE) took a leading role in the global campaign to force manufacturers to reduce their use of ozone depleting chemicals. About three years ago, the pressure group compiled a list of all companies known to be using CFCs and announced that it intended to make the list public. FOE claims that the threat made seven aerosol manufacturers agree to look for alternatives.

As part of the campaign, the group also organized an influential international conference on ozone depletion, attended by some of the world's leading scientists, in November 1988. This was followed by the launch of a campaign against the use of CFCs in the construction industry with the publication of the reports 'Safe as Houses' and 'Uses of CFCs in Buildings'. These reports were welcomed by the Royal Institute of Architects and others within the industry. The pressure group was also influential in the development of environmental policing.

Pippa Hyam, FOE's senior information officer, explains that although the campaign had been highly successful, the organization's next goal is for aerosols to be banned altogether: 'Aerosols are energy intensive and you can't throw them away. Alternative propellants also damage the atmosphere, albeit to a lesser extent.'

So Friends of the Earth is calling upon the British Aerosol Manufacturers Association (BAMA) and all manufacturers of aerosols containing the ozone depletant 1,1,1 trichloethane to commit themselves to a rapid phase out of this chemical. In its literature FOE lists the addresses, telephone numbers and details of the products of companies, who are using the chemical. She explains: 'We aim to educate people to make the changes themselves. Then, as industry responds, we move the goal posts. We would never be successful if we demanded a phase-out of aerosols immediately, but gradually we hope to stop their use.'

Case study: *3M*

Before 1988, 3M used ozone-depleting Arcton 12 and Arcton 13 at its factory in Gorseinon to expel air from aerosol cans before they were filled. Although 3M was under no legal obligation to stop its use of CFCs at this time, it installed a machine, which purged the empty cans by vacuum.

Annually the process has eliminated the use of 3.5 tonnes of CFCs and saved over £10,000. The initial capital outlay was a mere £5,000.

However, even this company – which is widely regarded as a leading light in pollution prevention, has encountered problems, from over-enthusiastic marketers. In late 1989 it was awarded Friends of the Earth's Green Con Award for labelling Scotch Spray Fix Protective Coating and Fixative and Scotch Spray Mount Adhesive with the slogan 'Does not contain propellants causing ozone depletion'. Both products contain 1,1,1 trichloroethane, also known as methyl chloroform, which, although it has a lower ozone depletion potential than CFCs, is produced and used in such large quantities that it is a major ozone depletant in its own right.

3M rapidly withdrew the claim and now simply states on the packaging that the product does not contain any CFCs.

In addition, it now has a policy to eliminate the use of 1,1,1 trichloroethane by the end of 1992.

Case study: *Iceland Frozen Foods*

Iceland has won a number of awards for its CFC initiatives. Whenever a customer buys a new refrigerator from Iceland, the company collects the old model free of charge and ensures that the harmful gases are removed safely. Most of the new models it sells have only half the volume of CFCs of those they replace. All of its coldstores operate on R22, which it describes as 'the most ozone friendly gas currently available for commercial use'.

Case study: *J. Sainsbury*

All Sainsbury's cold stores in distribution depots use HFC22 and since November 1989 all new and refurbished supermarkets use HFC22 as their only refrigerant. HFC22 is not controlled by the Montreal Protocol, which sets guidelines for CFC use. It has only 5% of the ozone depletion potential of commonly used refrigerants such as CFC12. Even so, the company is working with chemical manufacturers to develop alternative refrigerants, which will be totally ozone friendly.

In the meantime, Sainsbury uses electronic-leak detection as part of its store maintenance regime. The new Streatham Common supermarket has a unique coolant gas detection system, which automatically alerts both staff and the maintenance contractor if a leak should occur.

Sainsbury is also encouraging suppliers to conduct tests on CFC-free blown foam insulation materials for display cabinets and cold stores. When freezer equipment is disposed of, all existing refrigerants are decanted and returned to storage depots for re-use. This nationwide recycling service, established by Sainsbury with seven major refrigeration contractors, is believed to be the first of its kind.

Case study: *IBM UK*

IBM UK uses CFCs at its manufacturing sites as a cleaning solvent. According to an article in Personnel Management in April 1990, it has now set out to reduce its use of CFCs to 20% of its 1986 level by the end of 1992 – well in advance of the Montreal Protocol. IBM has also stopped using polystyrene cups and packaging, which use CFCs in their manu-facture. It no longer uses any CFC-based aerosols.

7.1.2.1 *Towards pollution free travel*

Every company can make a significant contribution to reducing air pollution by establishing environmentally aware travel policies. For example, car fleets, even of just two or three vehicles, can be converted to lead free petrol either immediately, if new, or when replaced. Enforcing this policy has cost benefits to the company, because lead free petrol is cheaper.

Many company cars are also fitted with catalytic convertors, which are designed to cut down on harmful emissions to an even greater extent. However, this will normally involve an investment, from which there is no direct payback, other than a recognition, from employees and customers, that the company is serious in its commitment to environmental issues.

Companies can also help reduce the volume of vehicles on the road by introducing car sharing schemes or by subsidizing employees' use of public transport. In many cases, this provides a useful additional recruitment incentive.

Oxford City Council has introduced bicycles for staff to use within the city, which has good cycle lanes and cycle filters at traffic lights. It only issues cars to staff, such as engineers, who need them to transport heavy equipment.

The London Borough of Sutton pays its staff the same mileage for bike and car use.

Case study: *British Telecom*

British Telecom staff provided the impetus behind its concerted effort to switch all cars to run on unleaded petrol.

It was a difficult task and serves as a valuable lesson for any company confronted with similar problems. BT has one of the largest and most varied fleets in Europe consisting of over 66,000 cars of all shapes and sizes. Most of them are models which are not capable of running con-tinuously on unleaded fuel. Obviously it would not have been com-mercially viable to replace them all at once. Even if the company had done so, the vehicles would have been passed onto new owners, who would still be driving on unleaded fuel.

Having decided that all cars bought in future would only run on unleaded petrol and having converted all the cars it could, BT still had 30,000 vehicles running on leaded fuel. It then set up a team to find a cheap way of running the remaining cars on unleaded petrol. The team found an inexpensive and permanent method of converting the cars which involved machining out old valve seats and replacing them with new hardened versions. British Telecom can now convert its entire vehicle fleet, at an acceptable cost, to run on unleaded petrol by 1991. A specially-trained team will carry out the conversions in each district. The engines will be stripped down in Telecom workshops and the cylinder heads sent away to have hardened valves fitted. The programme will cost over £3 million and pay for itself in a year and half thanks to the tax saving on unleaded fuel.

(Source: Personnel Management – April 1990)

Case study: *The Body Shop*

The Body Shop has converted all its company cars to run on lead-free petrol and all its new cars are fitted with three way catalytic convertors. In addition, the company is running trials with liquid petroleum gas, which does not produce any nitrogen oxide, lead, hydrocarbons or sulphur dioxide and costs a quarter of the price of ordinary petrol. The Body Shop also runs car-sharing schemes and is considering introducing company bicycles as a service-related benefit.

7.1.3 *Solid waste management*

The disposal of industrial waste threatens to become the major environmental issue of the 1990s in Britain. As landfill capacity shrinks, less suitable sites are being proposed and opposed; housing pressures, particularly in the South-East, are forcing the examination of old landfill sites, many of which are being rejected for building either because of dangerous build-up of methane, or because they contain toxic residues. Control over what companies can dump is likely to increase significantly during the next decade, forcing them to re-evaluate what waste products they produce and whether they could better invest resources in prevention, or recycling.

How can a company improve its waste management record? It can:
- encourage employees' suggestions for improvements
- look for opportunities to turn 'waste' into profitable by-products or recycle these materials
- monitor performance and make sure it is abreast of current technology
- employ an environment specialist to advise on waste disposal, possible future legislation and to maintain contact with appro-

priate trade associations – or seek help from its trade association, the CBI or qualified consultants
- publicize its environmental-improvement activities in the local media and among its staff

Other ideas include:
- pre-treating waste, to make it easier, safer, cheaper to get rid of or useful to another business
- thinking carefully about waste mixing – are you putting re-cyclable materials in with waste destined for landfill?
- refining your production process so that there is less waste to dispose of

Every aspect of company operations should be reviewed systematically. The CBI suggests organizations should look closely at:
- research and development
- planning of product or output
- design of manufacturing
- design of residuals
- design of waste handling facility to produce new resources from old residues
- design of the system as a whole to avoid waste.

In addition, manufacturing companies should also bear in mind that sooner or later plant will be shut down or they may want to move on. Now is the time to identify likely future problems from, for example, seepage of poisonous residues into the ground. The asset value of the site will be greatly reduced if it is contaminated. A gradual clean up over a period of several years of rebuilding will often be more cost-effective than tackling the whole site at a later date. As the principle 'Polluter pays' becomes increasingly applied, companies with this problem are likely to have no option but to clean up any sites, which they intend to dispose of or rebuild on.

Even office-based organizations can have a socially responsible waste management scheme. Employees can put all recyclable material such as paper, material and plastic into separate bins. To ensure that the collected rubbish does go to a recycling scheme, you can either allocate somebody within the company to be in charge of organising collection, or you can let your cleaning contractors take the materials to recycling points. Paper companies often pay for used paper in bulk volume, so the company need not incur additional cost penalties.

Case study: *Recycling City*

The Recycling City initiative demonstrated how reclamation industries, central and local government, the voluntary sector and other companies can form a successful recycling scheme.

A Friends of the Earth initiative, Recycling City was set up in Sheffield in the late 1980s. The paper industry provided some of the paper banks, which are located around the city and agreed to operate on a fixed price and guaranteed market.

Previously price fluctuations arising from instability in the paper market had meant local authorities often could not predict whether the income from collection would cover the costs.

The glass industry already had over 50 bottle banks in Sheffield, but it agreed to supply as many more as were required. It also agreed to buy all glass collected at a fixed price for the three years of the scheme.

Save a Can sited five containers on the edge of the city, whilst cans collected within the city were extracted from general rubbish by magnets at the city incinerator. The Aluminium Can Recycling Association provided promotional materials and assistance for schools and for voluntary sector collections. It offered target incentives such as bar magnets and hand operated crushers in addition to prizes for the highest per capita collection ratio. Both organizations have guaranteed a market price for materials reclaimed.

For the first time in the UK, the plastics industry committed itself to reclaiming from domestic refuse. The British Soft Drinks Association has provided 20 containers for the collection of transparent soft drinks bottles.

The British Plastics Federation installed five containers at civic amenity sites for heavy duty, opaque or coloured bottles. Support from the plastics industry was of major importance in the development of a comprehensive recycling strategy.

The oil industry worked with the council on a scheme which included siting oil recovery points in garages and local authority rubbish dumps.

Many voluntary groups were already running recycling schemes to raise money. These banded together to form the administrative unit SCRAP (Sheffield Community Action Recycling Programme). A grant from UK 2000 provided funds for a development worker to work for SCRAP for a year. After this the voluntary sector hoped to fund the post. The council also created the post of recycling officer to help co-ordinate the project.

A community enterprise set up weekly door to door collections to pick up recyclable waste from 10,000 households. The business then sold the collected glass, plastic, rags and paper. This operation, based on schemes in Germany and Canada, was the first of its kind in the UK. It aimed to recycle as much as possible by going to people such as housebound elderly, who found it difficult to get to the fixed point containers.

Recycling City admits that, 'Looked at in the narrowest terms, these rounds are barely economically viable. The amount of income received from collected materials hardly covers running costs and insufficient income is generated to invest in better vehicles, good publicity, and so on'. But, explains Pippa Hyam of Friends of the Earth: 'The collection rounds should be viewed in a much wider context than this narrow profit and loss definition. It costs disposal authorities a great deal of money to dump their waste. With the ever increasing pressure on landfill sites these costs will only increase. Each tonne of waste recycled means that the authorities will have less to deal with and this will reduce their costs.'

Dr Geoffrey Levy of Anglo-French packaging firm CMB is a representative at the newly-formed European Recovery and Recycling Association (ERRA). He points out the importance of the pressure group's efforts: 'We have nothing but praise for Friends of the Earth and the Recycling City initiative. They set up the project on a mininum amount of money and although it encountered a lot of problems, other projects can learn from their mistakes. ERRA is already sponsoring kerbside collection schemes in Sheffield and will be setting up its own pilot projects. It is the only forward for the packaging industry.'

Case study: *Superdrug*

Superdrug returns the hundreds of thousands of cardboard boxes received by each of its stores to central baling points, from where they are returned for recycling. The company estimates that this compressed cardboard waste will amount to 900,000 cubic feet in 1990. It is also looking at ways of recycling polythene packaging materials and has run a trial collection scheme, where customers can deposit used carrier bags in special bins in its stores.

Case study: *Allied Colloids*

Allied Colloids found it could minimize waste and save money at the same time.

The company supplies speciality chemicals to a wide range of industries. It produces liquid dispersion polymers, but the waste from this process when mixed with water forms a viscous sludge that is difficult to treat and dispose of.

In 1984, the company installed a settlement tank to extract the waste liquid, polymers and white spirit solvent before they became exposed to large amounts of waste water. The waste polymer and solvents are skimmed off and distilled. The five tonnes of white spirit annually recovered is reused. And the remaining polymer waste can be landfilled for £100 per tonne, as against the £500 per tonne it previously cost to dispose of both together. Moreover, as the waste polymer has been recovered before it absorbs too much water, the volume for disposal has been reduced from 20 tonnes to 10 tonnes per week.

The scheme has some major advantages. As well as reducing the amount of chemical that is sent to landfill, weekly disposal costs have been reduced from £10,000 to £1,000 and an additional saving of £1,000 a week is made on buying white spirit. The recovery plant, which cost about £25,000, is operated and maintained by one employee. And the payback period on the investment was less than three weeks.

Case study: *Dow Chemicals*

Dow Chemicals produces latex, agricultural chemicals and insulation materials at its 300-employee Kings Lynn plant.

The corporate waste minimization policy, 'Waste reduction always pays' (WRAP) has as its objectives to reduce waste, provide recognition for excellent performance in waste reduction, re-emphasize the need for continuous improvement and reduce long term waste management costs.

As part of the programme, Dow has made process modifications on its latex plants. Water hoses have been fitted with restriction nozzles to reduce the amount of water used. Water contaminated with latex is recycled. Water-cooled vacuum pumps have been replaced with double-sealed pumps, which eliminate the need for cooling water. A belt press dewatering unit has also been installed.

These modifications have led to a reduction in aqueous effluents and a 90% reduction in sludge sent to landfill. Disposal costs have been cut by approximately 70%.

Case study: *3M*

To minimise waste at its Aycliffe site, in 1988 3M introduced an innovative scheme to recycle polypropylene and polyester material.

Staff at Aycliffe make face masks and respirators. When they cut them out large amounts of cloth aren't used. In the past this was disposed to landfill, but in 1982 the company installed an incinerator to burn the material, which has a high calorific value.

Now the energy produced heats the plant and runs the machines. The incinerator works five days a week and is de-ashed on the sixth day.

In 1988 terms the capital cost of installation was £163,000. However with net operating savings of over £60,000 a year, the payback has been rapid. And the incinerator is estimated to have prevented over 250,000 tonnes of solid waste from going into landfill.

Case study: *Body Shop*

The Body Shop operates a major recycling programme, Project Paper-chase. All white and lightly coloured paper is segregated for collection by paper merchants for recycling. According to the company, this is not only environmentally responsible but raises awareness amongst staff and shows them the importance of individual effort. The company hopes they will become aware of implementing recycling at home.

The Body Shop is extending its direct link distribution from the ware-house to the shops for recovering certain plastic containers and cardboard boxes for re-use and recycling.

In the meantime, a number of shops in the chain have made arrange-ments with local charities, schools, and playgroups, who will collect cardboard boxes. Metal drums, used for transporting toiletries and cos-metics, are crushed and sent for recycling; large plastic drums are sluiced out and re-used. Smaller drums are often sold to fishermen for floats.

A recycling port for newspapers and aluminium is being set up at the organization's warehouse, for use by the local community and staff. Body Shop only uses recycled paper for note pads, re-usable sticky labels, photocopying paper, fax and even lavatory paper. The company is cur-rently trying to source recycled computer paper.

Although only 2% of customers bring in their empty bottles for refilling, the Body Shop still operates its longstanding refill policy.

The Body Shop has worked closely with Friends of the Earth since 1987 to raise public awareness on issues such as recycling waste as well as acid rain and ozone depletion. Jonathan Porritt, former director of the environmental pressure group said: 'Our link with the Body Shop has given us a shop window on the High Street.'

The Body Shop is also trying to find alternatives to plastic carrier bags. High density polyethylene film used to make till bags has been replaced by recycled paper. These bags carry informative environmental messages.

The status of the bio-degradable plastic carrier bag remains uncertain due to lack of hard evidence over its degradation in landfill conditions, and about possible harm that intermediate breakdown products may cause. A small carrier bag, made from bio-destructible plastic, in on trial.

Case study: *Friends of the Earth versus the supermarkets*

Environmental pressure group, Friends of the Earth, has campaigned successfully for recycled low grade toilet paper. Pippa Hyam, senior infor-mation officer at the London office, explains how its mobilization of consumer pressure made supermarkets change their policy: 'Toilet rolls have always had recycled high grade paper or pre-consumer waste in them. Following our first campaign, all companies did was stick a recycled label on the original product.'

'Our next target was to create a market for recycled paper made mainly from newspapers and magazines. Scout packs and environmental groups had been collecting newspapers for years and there was now a glut. So we set out to explain the need for a market for low grade paper. We held a day of action and local groups dressed as toilet rolls and stood outside supermarkets for the day. People were asked to sign petitions and hand them into the manager.'

Within a month certain supermarkets started marketing toilet rolls made from recycled low-grade paper.

She adds: 'It was a major victory. These retailers have to import low grade toilet paper from Holland, because British industry hasn't got the technology to product it yet. But we will continue to urge the build up of markets for low grade waste in a bid to prevent it being dumped into landfill.'

Checklist
1. Does your company know all the waste products it produces, in what amounts?
2. Does it have a formal system for identifying both potential and actual environmental impact?
3. Does it have a 'green' purchasing policy – and does it implement it strictly?
4. Does it actively seek ways to reduce both toxicity and volume of waste products? Docs it perceive this activity as a source of cost saving rather than a drain on resources?
5. Does it actively involve employees in monitoring environmental issues and suggesting improvements?
6. Does it have effective plans to minimise the damage from accidents?
7. Is it using the latest pollution prevention technology wherever possible? Does it have a programme to develop its own technology?

7.2 Energy conservation

'Global warming is a real threat. Therefore the time to do something is now.' The speaker is not a politician, nor a member of an environmental pressure group but Chris Hampson, executive director of Imperial Chemical Industries (ICI). Speaking in October 1989 at the Watt Committee on Energy, Hampson pointed out that analysis has shown that carbon dioxide in the atmosphere accounts for 50–60% of the Greenhouse Effect. Within this total, burning of fossil fuels such as coal, oil and gas, accounts for 40-45%.

So, explains Hampson, energy conservation is seven times more effective at reducing the major problem of CO_2 emissions than other supply options. Moreover, it is known to work.

He cites the figures:
'In 21 countries belonging to the International Energy Agency, economic output grew on average by 32% between 1973 and 1986, and yet energy demand rose by just five per cent. In the US, which consumes a quarter of the world's fuels, the annual demand for energy is still below that of 1973 even though the country's GDP is up by 40%. Similiar figures are available for Japan.'

He suggests three routes to follow:
1. Improved fuel and energy conservation in new or existing power generation facilities
2. More general energy saving programmes for public electricity consumption
3. Specific energy conservation projects in the major power consuming industries.

He rounds off: 'Energy conservation is not the only way to resolve the environmental issues around energy generation and use, but it is something that we can practise now and where the effects can be predicted with confidence.'

The Association for the Conservation of Energy concurs, listing three important sectors where attention to detail could have an effect:
• commercial lighting
• industrial motors
• domestic refrigerators/freezers.

These three sectors account for more than 42% of total electricity used. In lighting alone, which accounts for 15% of total energy at a cost of £1.6 billion a year, energy consumption could be halved by new technologies such as high frequency lamps and occupancy sensors.

The government also recognizes the problem and has been running a campaign since 1983 through its Energy Efficiency Office. Its target is to reduce energy consumption by 20% from current levels.

Energy costs also have a direct bearing on bottom line profitability. So what can a company do to ensure it is cutting back on fuel consumption (and bills)? Among the options are:

1. Conduct an energy audit
2. Install low energy lighting on timers
3. Use energy more than once – for example, refrigerators use a lot of energy, but they also give off heat. Can this be used to heat the plant/shop/office?
4. Install occupancy sensors
5. Educate the workforce – publish posters and leaflets explaining why energy conservation is important.

Case study: *Wessex Water*

Wessex Water's Avonmouth works produces methane gas from sewage sludge in sufficient quantitity to heat and power the treatment works. This is a considerable achievement since energy is a substantial part of the company's operating costs. The scheme is so succesful that any surplus electricity generated is sold to the local electricity board.

During 1988-89, the works won a South West Electricity Board Gold Award for its economic use of energy in relation to sludge disposal.

Case study: *ICI*

'ICI generates an eighth of the British private energy supply and our energy bill is about the same as we spend on salaries and wages,' confides executive director Chris Hampson.

The UK Chemical industry is the third biggest consumer of industrial energy users, yet it represents only 10 per cent of the manufacturing output of the UK. So ICI is under considerable pressure to work towards energy conservation.

In 1983, ICI Fertilisers decided to replace its two oldest plants at Severnside in Bristol. ICI built a new, smaller plant that could match the output and energy efficiency of its best capacity plants. The new plant, which used new technology based on advanced engineering and modern distributed control systems, required only half the amount of steel for its construction. It also achieves a reduction of 60% CO_2 and 75% reduction of ammonia in liquid effluent compared with conventional ammonia plants.

Another example is the production of chlorine, a basic building block in today's chemical industry. In the 1970s, the most widely-used process for electrolysis of brine to make chlorine was the mercury cell. This is highly energy intensive and the mercury is recognised as an environmental hazard.

ICI explored alternative technologies and came up with a non-mercury membrane electrolyser, the FM21 cell. This is available from ICI on licence and has now been introduced into more than 20 plants throughout the world. Its power requirement is over 20% lower per tonne than the mercury cell.

The company is also looking at building a combined heat and power plant, based on natural gas at Teeside. The plant would provide energy for ICI's own use and the remainder would be sold to the UK market.

The waste heat would supply the total steam requirements of the complex, replacing the present coal-fired facilities.

Case study: *J. Sainsbury*

Sainsbury's began its energy-saving programme in earnest in 1974 and has since won a number of awards for energy efficiency. For example, a new store near Guildford won the Electricity Council's 1989 Beta award.

The store uses recycled heat from refrigeration plants. Use of such new technology, combined with radical changes in lighting, environmental control and refrigeration has meant that Sainsbury's supermarkets use only 60% of the energy that they would have 10 years ago.

Checklist
1. Does your company monitor energy usage in its buildings and equipment?
2. Does it have an active programme of energy saving?
3. Does it encourage employees to save energy, e.g. through car-pooling?
4. Does it take energy-saving factors into account when building/buying new plants/premises?

7.3 Urban renewal

Environmental improvement is an issue that many companies have tackled. They have set about solving the problem of rundown inner city areas, urban degeneration and conservation in a variety of ways, but most commonly by forming partnerships to tackle the problem. The first partnership was in Calderdale and had the firm backing of HRH The Prince of Wales, who has been in support of the idea from the outset.

The partnership, backed by Business in the Community, brought together a focus group from the public and private sectors, to pursue practical projects ranging from environmental improvements through to business expansion, educational experiments, and a major industrial development.

This started the trend for a series of business partnership initiatives in areas such as Newcastle, Bristol, Nottingham and Teeside.

Enterprise agencies have also been instrumental in developing urban renewal programmes.

Companies which do not want to join a large partnership arrangement can always set up their own projects for improving their surroundings. Some companies put money into local conservation projects or give regular sums to the National Trust or other conservation organisations.

Other companies try to site their new buildings on derelict or rundown land, landscaping and planting trees in the area at the same time as building. A construction company has encouraged urban renewal by lending its expertise to help people build themselves a new home and a new life in the inner city.

Every organization can find a way of improving the environment for the community. It is an obvious and highly visual way of enchancing its reputation with the general public.

Case study: *J. Sainsbury plc*

Over half of Sainsbury's stores built since 1986 have used derelict or rundown urban sites. Sainsbury's also chooses sites, which are unsuited to other types of development, because they are close to motorways or railways.

The company believes in a comprehensive approach to landscape design that recognizes the obligation of a new development to its local environment.

To this end it employs some of the country's leading landscape architects and supports each scheme with a long term aftercare programme or regular maintenance.

Wherever possible, the company uses existing trees, bushes and shrubs to provide scale and shelter. It also mass-plants young trees and shrubs as well as semi-mature trees.

The company supports Green Belt policy and will not seek planning permission on Green Belt land. In rural sites, it has given land to nature conservancy and it has also retained local wildlife and habitat where possible.

In some developments, tree surgeons, employed by the company, have moved existing trees using modern technology and successfully kept them alive and healthy.

Case study: *British Telecom*

After flotation, British Telecom undertook a major internal study on the role of the company within the context of inner cities. As they became aware of the severity of rising unemployment, a decline in manufacturing capacity and depressed housing conditions, the board members decided to create a community action budget to tackle the issues.

During 1989 and 1990 British Telecom provided financial support for more than 90 projects. These fall into three categories:
- resources for training schemes for the long term unemployed, women returners, and disabled people. In many cases BT has provided the start up costs for training schemes and the government or the Training Agency has met the day to day expenditure.
- enterprise training and the provision of small workspaces for new businesses. Working with inner city task forces or voluntary agencies, BT has provided capital to convert disused buildings into enterprise centres where young people have a base to start commercial activities. An integral part of these centres is enterprise training sessions. Youngsters are trained in marketing, accounting and other related subjects. BT supports inner city projects to reclaim industrial wasteland and peripheral housing estates. It also works with social workers and youth organizations to set up community improvement schemes in these areas.
- social welfare programmes. In some areas, BT gives a grant to help community development; in others it funds a community worker. It particularly favours community computer centres, where local people develop community services and acquire basic computer skills. The company has also provided practical support in developing leadership teams in major provincial cities. The teams work with local authorities and government departments to develop economic policies by attracting inward investment and acting as catalysts for development and construction.

The criteria for making grants are under constant review so that they reflect the changing economic position and demands of society. In almost every case, British Telecom acts alongside other organizations, such as Business in the Community, and in some cases with other companies. It recognizes that the long term solution to our inner city problems cannot be solved by any one agency but only through partnerships.

Case study: *Rosehaugh plc*

Construction company Rosehaugh helps people to build their own homes under its self-build scheme.

The first scheme is on an empty site in Bethnal Green, East London, which was made available by the Borough Council of Tower Hamlets.

Land costs, which often constitute half the value of a new house, have been lowered by a new approach to land tenure. The landowner makes land available on commercial terms by granting a 99 year lease to self-build associations without any initial payment. The landowner receives ground rent or a capital sum if the self builder decides to buy the freehold.

Godfrey Bradman, chairman and joint executive, developed the idea after a discussion with the Prince of Wales about the inadequate house stock in Britain and the consequent long waiting lists for public housing. The scheme, financed by the Halifax Building Society, was launched by the Prince in 1988.

The self-builders are contracted to provide a minimum of 26 hours work each week for a 12 to 15 months. Some members are skilled in the building trade while other memebers of the team are electricians and plumbers.

Rosehaugh is examining the potentially wider application of the idea to help young homeless people, prisoners reaching the end of their sentence and the disabled.

Case study: *Blackburn Partnership*

Blackburn Partnership was launched by the Prince of Wales in 1988 to bring together the public and private sectors to attract jobs to the Blackburn area.

Fundamental issues for the regeneration of the area are improving the environment, removal or improvement of substandard housing, attracting office developments to Blackburn and the reduction of unemployment.

Companies such as British Aerospace/Royal Ordnance and ICI have committed well over £250,000 towards the largest Groundwork Trust in the country. The trust includes among its projects, a refurbishment of frontages in Darwen town centre and the restoration of Daisyfield Mill on the canal in Blackburn. The Blackburn Partnership is concentrating on improving the environment because it believes better surroundings inevitably contribute to an improved quality of life, which in turn can attract investment to the area.

The Lancashire Evening Telegraph, Crown Berger and the Tidy Britain campaign run Grimewatch to pick up litter and generally tidy up run down areas of the town. The newspaper features the campaign's activities daily. According to the partnership brochure, the campaign has been an enormous success.

The partnership has also welded links between a number of organizations to lobby for early construction of an M6/M65 motorway link and a Blackburn inner relief road to improve the infrastructure.

The borough council, Norwest Holst Partnerships Ltd, North British Housing Association and Northern Counties Housing Association have combined efforts to provide much needed housing for sale and rent in the Brookhouse area.

Tackling unemployment and stimulating new jobs in the service sector are two of the partnership's key objectives. It has created an export textile co-operative in Brookhouse, helping small and medium sized companies export to Europe, and, in the Prince's Trust Community Venture, provides youngsters with valuable work experience.

Following a suggestion by The Prince of Wales that the scheme should market itself more effectively, the Borough Council gave £100,000 to a specially formed company, Blackburn Marketing Ltd. A local employer has lent a secondee to help run this new organisation.

Checklist
1. Do you support
   - local/national nature conservation groups?
   - partnership agreements for urban regeneration?
2. When considering a new site are environmental/landscaping issues a factor?
3. Do you have a policy against Green Belt planning applications?
4. Could you band together with several local companies and other agencies to set up an environmental improvement scheme for your area?

7.4 Environmental auditing

'In the UK, the Environment Protection Bill is now proceeding at speed through parliament. It will improve and tighten up environmental legislation and make it more imperative than ever that businesses look closely at how they relate to the environment, and put in management systems and technologies to reduce their impact on it,' said the CBI at a conference on environmental auditing in June 1990. It estimates: 'All businesses are affected by the environment debate, but to date only relatively few are using the systematic approach which an environmental audit offers.'

Martin Charter, managing director of KPH Marketing, a company that specializes in environmental audits, endorses this view. 'Within the UK, environmental auditing is a relatively new discipline outside the oil, chemical and pharmaceutical industries. There have been an estimated two hundred completed projects to date. However, decision makers across industry are now coming under a variety of pressures to establish an environmental policy. An environmental audit is a necessary precursor for this.

'By taking a broad view of environmental auditing and by understanding its interconnections both in and outside the organisation, companies will be able to generate creative, cost reducing and revenue generating ideas, that will have a direct impact on the bottom line.

'Senior management must face this responsibility and champion the change and empower management and staff to implement the new policies. The results are likely to improve morale, produce a better corporate image and ultimately improve market share and profitability.'

An environmental audit explores all aspects of a company's manufacturing, office and field safety procedures and attempts to:
– analyse its effect on the environment
– suggest ways of minimizing its effect.

Although, like a financial audit, it provides a snap-shot of the organization at one time, the environmental audit is different in that it is intended to force positive change. Attention is directed not simply to the environmental bottom line, but to every point where the organization may have a negative impact on the environment.

For most companies, an audit will reveal areas, where action is needed, either in terms of policy formulation, or preventive implementation. Top management must become involved at this point, to set priorities and establish broad budgets.

European Community legislation may well make environmental audits obligatory for public companies, over the next few years. Those companies which invest in auditing systems while it is still voluntary, stand to gain significant benefits in terms of market positioning.

Case study: *Allied Signal*

Based in the USA Allied Signal is a major manufacturing corporation with over 240 plants worldwide and over 11,000 employees working in the automotive, aerospace and engineered materials sector. In 1978 upon the recommendation of an outside consultant, it embarked on a 'Health, Safety and Environmental Surveillance Programme'.

The programme's purpose was to ensure compliance with existing legislation and check that operating companies were able to comply with future standards.

The audit function is carried out by the Corporate Health, Safety and Environmental Sciences Department. Within this 14 person team are three full time environmental auditors, one each for health, safety and the environment. The department is headed by a vice president reporting to the senior vice president of operating services.

The audit covers seven areas:

- air pollution control
- water pollution and spill prevention
- solid waste disposal
- occupational health
- medical programmes
- safety and loss prevention
- product safety.

From an annual budget of US$ 750,000, the company conducts fifty audits annually, a sample of about three per cent. Each audit covers one of the three areas.

Audited sites are chosen from each of the corporation's main business areas and operating companies. Facility managers are notified of a review one month in advance.

Each audit team uses techniques such as formal audit protocols, written questionnaires, informal interviews with key members of staff, physical measurement and documentation checks. An audit takes around four days. The team then issues a written report in draft for the facility manager and line and corporate staff, followed by a final report which takes into account any comments.

The facility manager has to prepare a written response to this report within one month and draw up and execute an action plan to remedy any deficiencies noted. About 20% of these action plans are followed up again by the audit team.

The company places environmental responsibility with sector presidents. Each year they must write an environmental assurance letter, guaranteeing that appropriate health, safety and environmental systems are in place and working. They must also state that any deficiencies are being dealt with – and how.

Allied Signal is making a substantial effort to keep its business practices both within and in advance of legislation. Because legislature requirements vary from country to country, it aims to use the strictest requirements as the corporate standard. Nonetheless, the sheer size of the auditing task means that the process is mainly reactive rather than proactive.

This case study was provided by Matthew Nicol of Bioscan (UK) Ltd and Martin Charter of KPH Marketing Ltd who have formed a working partnership to examine corporate environmental stances from audit through to implementation.

Case study: *Texaco*

Texaco has introduced regular audits, involving rigorous checks for air, water and solid waste pollution, at all UK operational sites.

In addition, particularly hazardous substances such as asbestos and PCBs will be monitored.

Auditors check that staff are prepared for any foreseeable emergency and that they comply with safety regulations, company policy and legislation. They will draw up a plan of action for any deficiences noted.

The audit programme, which began at Sunderland in January 1990, will improve Texaco's environmental image, according to Brian Keal, manager of safety and environmental affairs.

The auditors' findings are discussed with site managers before they depart and followed up subsequently with a re-audit. Audits will also be carried out before the company buys and sells land. Environmental complaints will be thoroughly investigated, with adequate clean-up procedures following any cases of contamination.

When the safety and environmental affairs department was created in 1989, Texaco became one of the first major oil companies to appoint a director, Brian Goodland, with sole responsibility for this area.

Checklist
1. Does your company hold regular environmental audits? If so, is there any procedure in place to follow an audit up?
2. Do you publicize positive developments to employees/the general public?

8 How to organise social responsibility activities

Social responsibility doesn't just happen. It has to be made to happen, through commitment at the top and innovation and initiative at the bottom. Every company will want to arrange its social responsibility function differently, according to its own priorities, but it will need at a minimum:
• a system to generate and review social responsibility policies at the highest level and, in most cases, at individual business level
• a system for gathering information about social responsibility trends and about the organisation's performance
• a system for stimulating change and, where necessary, for enforcing it.

8.1 Organising at board level

Responsibility for everything that happens within a company starts with the board.

In reviewing the social responsibility of a wide variety of companies, we have observed that a major limiting factor is often the dispersion of responsibilities. Because concern for different areas of social responsibility action has arisen at different times and within different business functions, it is hardly surprising, for example, to find there is little co-ordination in many companies between purchasing policy and environmental policy. This normally has to be done at functional level rather than at organisational level.

Although chemical and manufacturing companies, for example, often have a board member responsible for co-ordinating all environmental policies, few companies have a board member who is responsible for all social responsibility activities. One of the widest briefs our research identified was that of Trevor Toolan, BR's managing director, personnel, who is responsible for the activity of British Rail's community unit. His brief touches on purchasing policy, conservation and the environment as well as education, the arts, fundraising and urban regeneration projects.

However, it does not cover other areas such as customer service.

One of the best ways to organise social responsibility issues is to have regular meetings between function heads, who report to a board member responsible for social responsibility. The allocated director takes charge of ensuring that the company activities in this field are documented and publicized.

The board should also be responsible for developing and implementing a general code of practice and for ensuring that all divisions and businesses both apply it and develop their own, subsidiary versions, adapted to their particular needs.

Our case studies show how some companies organise various social responsibility affairs at board level. None of them have a board director in charge of *all* social responsibility issues, although some have fairly wide briefs.

Case study: *Marks and Spencer*

Marks and Spencer's policy is to support the communities in which the company trades. It commits over £5 million annually to this community involvement programme, via a community involvemnt committee, which includes five main board directors. Three specialist sub-committees, each chaired by a director, deal with health care; the arts; and community services, which include education, training and secondment.

Case study: *IBM*

IBM allocates community investment resources through a planning process, which begins in March each year and leads up to an approved plan for the following year by about October. The plan, which covers resource usage at central, regional and local level is reviewed and approved by IBM UK's management committee, consisting of the chief exective and his reporting directors. Throughout the year, the management committee regularly reviews progress. The board discusses the plan at least once a year.

Case study: *Allied Dunbar*

Allied Dunbar has set up a community affairs department and delegated community affairs away from the board.

Annual reports from the Allied Dunbar Charitable Trust state: 'Responsibility and accountability for our community affairs activities have been delegated away from the board. Having made the important decisions in respect of principles, general direction, and resources to be made available, directors rely on trustees, in conjunction with professional staff and advisors, to develop and implement appropriate programmes.

Case study: *ICI*

ICI's board has prime responsibility for determining environmental policy. To assist the board, the chairman has nominated an executive director to take a group overview of safety, health and environmental matters.

The principal executive officers of the international businesses, who are directly accountable to the ICI board, are responsible for establishing environmental standards for their businesses in line with group environmental policy.

In ICI, chief executive officers are responsible for territories. The chief executive officer in each regional ICI subsidiary company, together with its board, is responsible for establishing, implementing and monitoring environmental policy for that company, consistent with local laws and with standards set by principal executive officers.

8.2 Organizing at business function level

Expecting one individual to be an expert in say, both customer service issues and pollution control isn't realistic. So companies with effective programmes set up specialist teams in the critical areas for their business. These will tend to cover some or all of the headings we have used in this guide:

- customer service
- personnel and training
- supplier management and purchasing
- environment
- public affairs/lobbying
- sponsorship and charitable giving.

The titles will differ, as will the combinations of responsibility, but the objectives are common – to monitor and police every aspect of the company's activities within that part of the social responsibility framework.

The danger is that some key areas will fall through the cracks. Who, for example, takes responsibility for guaranteeing that the company's marketing practices are ethical and honest? Once again, it is the responsibility of the board to ensure that each of the social responsibility teams has clear written guidelines, job descriptions/mission statements and targets; and to pull those together to ensure that every social responsibility area is adequately covered.

In the following section we describe how some leading edge

companies have tackled this level of social responsibility organisation.

8.2.1 *Organising giving*

'A corporate community affairs programme is not a distraction from the serious business of running a commercial enterprise. It is actually part of the enterprise and is as important as other ancillary service areas, such as public relations departments. If it is well managed, it will not only make a real contribution to the community but will in the process enhance the reputation of the enterprise', Joel Joffe, deputy chairman of Allied Dunbar, told Business in the Community Magazine in Spring 1989.

But to have a successful community involvement policy, a company must:
- decide primary aims of policy
- select areas it is going to support and formulate a written policy
- decide on criteria for beneficiary organisations
- state clearly what it will *not* support
- allocate a person/set up a department responsible for giving
- ensure the community involvement department reports regularly to the board.

In addition as Joffe points out, a company should be:
- defining objectives – clear objectives must be agreed reflecting exactly what the company hopes to achieve from the programme
- fixing budgets – a decision on the amount of the budget, preferably for an ongoing amount determined without annual reference to the board. A measure satisfactory to many companies is a fixed percentage of the profits
- delegating – delegate responsibility and accountability away from the the board. The board should be informed periodically of progress as in other areas of the company.

Joffe also suggests that grants to voluntary organisations are formalized into negotiated agreements so that reasons for support are clear and the objectives and targets of the organisation are also stated.

Identifying and categorising potential recipients of donations can be a time-consuming task, fraught with value judgements. Although value judgements will always be present, it is possible to reduce their impact by imposing formal methods of analysis. One proposed some years ago by one of the authors is the *Giving Matrix*.

The axes of the matrix are:
- value/benefit to the company
- value/benefit to the community.

Using Delphi techniques, simple questionnaires, or preset criteria developed from the overall giving objectives, the company can fairly rapidly identify those opportunities which will be of significant mutual benefit.

A low score for the company, but high for the community will trigger the question 'Is this something we should support just because no-one else will?'

A high score for the company but not for the community indicates that this is something for a different budget – probably marketing.

A low score on both axes automatically rules a project out.

The Giving Matrix: 1

```
                    |
        10          |
                    |
Value/benefit       |
to the company      |
                    |
            1       |_____  10
                    Value/benefit
                    to the community
```

A high score on both counts means that the project should move to the next stage. Here the two axes of the matrix become overall benefit and cost.

The Giving Matrix: 2

```
                    |
        10          |
                    |
Benefit             |
                    |
            1       |_____  10
                        Cost
```

Clearly, the lower the cost and the higher the benefit, the more attractive the project will be.

Of course, these broadbrush evaluation techniques cannot give the whole picture and the organization will normally wish to take into account other factors, such as implementability, whether the project is local or not, and timing. Nonetheless, the disciplined approach is a useful means of filtering out the mass of requests in a fair and logical manner.

Case study: *Marks and Spencers*

The company commits over £4 million every year to its community involvement programme. This includes cash contributions and over 20 members of staff who are full time seconded to a wide range of charitable organisations, job creation and youth training schemes.

The community affairs department has 12 employees who handle over 8000 requests a year. The team also assists many organisations by giving them guidance on fund raising and management techniques.

Stores are encouraged to help decide which local charities to give money to. Each store has funds available to support local appeals. In addition, staff often raise considerable sums for their favourite charities.

Stores support those charities, which do not usually generate major public support, but which reflect the needs of the communities where it has stores. Often it hands over seed corn money to help a deserving project get started.

Job creation, youth training, education, health and projects for those with special needs and elderly are included in the brief. The company also sponsors the arts and local events.

It does not support overseas projects, political organisations, animal welfare charities, individuals, sports (except for the disabled), capital and endowment funding, third party funding or major national charities except in special circumstances.

Case study: *Barclays Bank*

Barclays receives over 40,000 requests for money a year. Through experience it has found that a good way of coping with the demand is for the bank to actually select and vet charities themselves and then offer them money rather than wait for letters to come through the post.

Brian Carr, head of Barclay's community enterprise unit, and his 14 strong team have shortlisted over 65 charities that fell within their brief to support the disabled, the disadvantaged, the young, the old and the handicapped.

Then they researched the charity's effectiveness by looking at the administration and balance sheets over a period of years as well as statistical analysis of how many people the charity has actually helped. If the charity passes the test, Carr approaches it and asks if there are any projects that the bank can sponsor.

He says: 'This way, we believe we are using our funds more efficiently and we are also encouraging the charity to run more effectively.'

He adds: 'We have found that some charities spend 80% of their time running around in circles doing administration and not actually helping anyone. We are making giving more professional.'

In 1987 Barclays ranked third in the league table of 400 community and charity donors companies. Carr says: 'These days it is not enough just to do good, you have to be seen to be doing good in the community and that is what we try to achieve.'

Among Barclays' policy decisions are to give where the benefits can be clearly seen and to avoid political issues. Carr explains: 'We like to give money to charities directly rather than to third parties, e.g Rotary. Equally we would not give to a local action group since they could be protesting against the activities of one of our customers.' He adds: 'It is our customers who provide our profits, and without profits we cannot support the community.'

Neither will Barclays fund individuals or certain charities which already have strong support. Brian says: 'We try to support the underdog. The charities that aren't popular. Somebody has got to help these people and we believe that it is the right thing to do. The tradition goes back to the nineteenth century. We don't have responsibility to the rich chairmen of multinationals, but we do have to help the old and others who can't help themselves.'

Case study: *Allied Dunbar Assurance*

Allied Dunbar has a team of nine people working in its community affairs department. Five specialists in related fields have been recruited to define, implement and accept responsibility for the funding policies and other programmes.

Joel Joffe, deputy chairman, points out: 'A community affairs department needs to be staffed by experienced professionals in the same way as any other specialist department. In order to manage an effective programme, the same approach must be followed as in managing the rest of the company.'

This would include:
– defining objectives
– fixing budgets
– delegation away from the board
– the creation of a community affairs department.

Allied Dunbar has four separate staff charity funds: one for the London employees; another for those who work in Swindon; and a foundation for the mobile sales force. In addition it has a separate charity for Isle of Man employees. Staff choose the main themes for giving – such as handicapped adults, older people, children and the Third World. They contribute through covenants and fund raising events. The Swindon-based staff charity fund raises more than £150,000 annually, with the company itself giving £2,000 per year towards running costs and administrative support from the community affairs department.

The fund is administered by a main committee with representatives from each department. All applications are thoroughly investigated including site visits in their own and the company's time.

The staff come from all levels within the company and many find that the involvement helps them to develop new and existing skills such as team work, committee chairing, report writing and decision making.

Allied Dunbar also issues a comprehensive annual report, listing all donations. The report for 1989 is available from the Community Affairs Department. It also produces a publications list with over 20 items which covers articles on the practice and theory of corporate community involvement.

8.2.2 *Organising environmental control*

For obvious reasons, companies leading the field in environmental awareness tend to come from the manufacturing sector, although the proportion of service company organizations with active involvement is steadily rising. The key in either sector is to have a coherent environmental policy. Manufacturing companies which wish to improve their environmental performance should ensure that that they:

- employ an environmental expert
- set up a department responsible for environmental issues
- join relevant trade organisations
- ensure the firm backing of the board and senior management
- issue a short environmental mission statement – operating companies and subsidaries will formulate their own based on it
- update equipment with best available environmental technology. Companies that design their own equipment should introduce environmental criteria to the design process
- issue a newsletter to employees informing them of the company's commitment and raise their awareness of the issue; offer awards for any environmental improvements they may suggest.

Other businesses can:
- formulate a brief environment policy statement to show commitment to staff, shareholders and the general public.

- allocate a member of staff to be responsible for general environmental matters
- set up staff award schemes for new environmentally-friendly ideas
- only use reycled paper
- use environmentally-friendly cleaning agents
- ensure that all new products bought for the business have the best available environmental technology
- publicise the company's efforts in the annual report/company magazine.

Case study: 3M

John Elkington, author of 'The Green Consumer Guide' is unequivocal about 3M's environmental performance: 'Without a shadow of a doubt, the most impressive environmental success story has starred 3M.'

The reason for its outstanding success is that the programme has the firm backing of senior management. Chairman of the environment council is Dr Richard Smith. The council includes five directors. Formed in late 1989, it meets every six weeks and enables senior managers from public relations, personnel, research, marketing, distribution, engineering and manufacturing departments as well as the healthcare division to monitor environmental issues. The council sets quantitative targets, monitors progress, establishes responsibility and identifys areas for action. Line managers then have responsibility for working out detailed action plans and reporting on progress.

The UK environment committee is unique in 3M. It creates a forum for focussing attention on environmental issues and stimulates a climate in which these issues can be positively addressed.

All employees can win an award entitled the 'Bond of Excellence' for ideas, effort or outstanding service. Staff are awarded with a bond which is equivalent to one share.

For example, the secretary who introduced 'green bins' into the Bracknell offices early in 1990 would be likely to receive this recognition. The bins only contain recyclable paper and the 'green' bags are picked up separately by the refuse collectors.

As consumer pressure intensified, 3M brought in an extension of the 3P programme in 1988. Says Smith: 'This project is called 3P Plus and places more emphasis on environmental benefits than on cost saving. Originally environmental projects had to stand alone and pay for themselves. Under the extended initiative, the projects have to make some saving, but cost saving is not the prime purpose.'

Case study: *CMB Packaging*

CMB was created by the merging of two international packaging leaders, Groupe Carnaud and Metalbox Packaging. CMB Packaging is the holding company of one of the largest packaging groups in the world. It is the European leader with factories in all the major EEC countries as well as operations in North and South America, Africa, the Middle East and the Asia Pacific region.

CMB produces metal, plastic packaging and paper board for the food, drink, pharmaceutical, cosmetic, household and industrial markets. It currently operates with 145 factories in 21 countries, employing over 37,000 people worldwide with a turnover in excess of £2 billion.

The environmental affairs department was set up in 1989 when the two companies merged. Dr Geoffrey Levy heads a small team which has to develop and publish an overall mission and policy statement and a strategic action programme which will include an environmental audit of the company's operations. In addition, each separate business within the company has somebody, often the managing director, who is responsible for environmental issues. The team must also be aware of legislation in all the territories and make sure that the company is not only adhering to statutes, but also one step ahead.

Levy explains: 'CMB has always been an ethical company. We always position ourselves well inside what is acceptable.But since emission legislation is about to be tightened up, we must be even more stringent and look at how we can improve environmental controls.'

The department's umbrella statement is tight: 'CMB regards overall environmental awareness and understanding by its employees and other partners to be the key in taking responsible action to achieve excellence. The strategy is to identify and address the real issues.' Each business has the option to write its own statement, applicable directly to its operations.

CMB also aims to raise the general environmental consciousness among employees through a regular newsletter 'Environment Today' and a database which the decentralised operations can read and add current research and news items to. Levy explains that the database and briefing documents are significant factors in keeping employees abreast of environmental issues, as the various operations are spread over the world. He added: 'The newsletter deals with general environmental problems such as recycling. With the newsletter and the environmental database, we want to make our employees aware that their company cares about the environment and hopefully encourage them to automatically take the environment into consideration when coping with everyday problems.'

One of the department's key tasks is to support industry initiatives at a national and international level. Levy is a vice chairman of the European

Recovery and Recycling Association which was formed in late 1989. ERRA was established by 19 major international companies to promote and accelerate the resolution of solid waste recycling problems.

By combining the resources and expertise of its members with those of the scientific community, industrial institutions and waste management specialists, ERRA can support major practical projects and is also well placed to sponsor scientific research and provide an authoritative information source. Alongside Nestle, the Coca Cola Company, Proctor and Gamble and L'Oreal, CMB is putting large sums of money into this initiative. These companies believe that the recovery and recycling of materials from household waste will be tackled most effectively if companies pool their expertise and money.

Levy is also chairman of the European Metal Packaging Environment Commission (SEFEL). Nationally, CMB is a part of the British Plastics Federation, the Metal Packaging Manufacturers Association and supports Incpen, the Industrial Council for Packaging and the Environment. The company also supports The Tidy Britain Group. Explains Levy: 'Packaging is perceived by some as an environmental problem because it has high visibility and is the ultimate symbol of the throwaway society. In reality it is an essential and beneficial service and helps make effective use of energy and raw materials. The modern supermarket could not exist without today's packaging, a lot of food would be damaged in transit and the rest would have to be bought and eaten immediately. Nevertheless the public sees us as partly responsible for the litter problem, so we have to be seen to help.'

Individual operations also run their own recycling initiatives. And in the packaging technology centre at Wantage, staff are encouraged to bring in empty bottles and containers to be used in recycling research.

8.2.3 *Organizing other functions*

Much the same principles apply to organizing other functions which have a social responsibility dimension. Critical in each case is:
- a direct (two-way) line to top management
- a broad enough control structure to ensure that the same people are not acting as both poacher and game-keeper.

For example, while the purchasing department may carry out the mechanics of monitoring the company's behaviour towards suppliers, it should not be the sole judge of its own performance. Other departments with an interest (personnel and production, for example) should be included on the controlling committee, both to ensure that *their* interests are taken care of and to provide a different perspective. If the company has the courage to invite suppliers, too, to join the committee, then so much the better.

8.3 The ethical foundation

The dispersion of responsibility for social responsibility issues inevitably opens the door for contradictory decisions and behaviours in different parts of the organization. To a considerable extent the cure for this lies in a high level of top management involvement. But two other mechanisms can help:
• deliberately opening up the ethics debate as another area where consensus is valued
• a broad code of practice to specify the organization's attitudes and values.

8.3.1 *Opening the debate*

Research into 'corporate deviance' in the United States suggests that managers often operate with split personalities. On the one hand, they are pillars of the community, model parents and good churchgoers. On the other, they are prepared to make decisions on behalf of their company, that they would condemn in their other persona. At its extreme, this phenomenon results in illegal activities, such as price rigging cartels, falsifying research results or overcharging clients. The motivation for this behaviour appears to stem from group loyalty – in itself a valuable and commendable attribute *within proper bounds*.

One of the keys to ensuring that managers do behave ethically is to make it clear that ethical considerations should be the same inside and outside the organization. Among specifics the company can employ are:

• *Ethical training*
Training managers in how to tackle decisions ethically builds the language and perspectives of social responsibility into the company. In this way, every department from purchasing to public affairs and personnel will take the same basic factors into consideration.

MacDonald and Zepp of the University of Macau have researched how companies tackle ethics training – in an article for Management Decision 28,1, they report that the following training techniques have been helpful:
– question and answer sessions to define people's views and challenge their reasoning

– open discussion groups
– the use of employees' own examples to show conflict and ethical dilemmas
– the expression of a full range of ethical views.

Case study: *Allied Signal*

In the mid 1980s, Allied Signal, a major manufacturing organization, was one of the first US companies to run an internal training programme specifically devoted to the subject of ethics. Allied Signal now devotes three days a year per manager to an ethical training programme.
   This programme has three specific objectives:
– to enable managers to recognise ethical decisions
– having recognised them, to decide what to do about them
– to learn how to anticipate emerging ethical issues.

The Chicago Mercantile Exchange gives its members two hour ethics classes in the wake of financial scandals, which emerged at the end of the bull run in American financial markets in the 1980s.

● *Appointing an ethics ombudsman*
MacDonald and Zepp suggest creating the post of ethical ombuds-person to guide employees on ethical questions. They state:
● an ombudsperson should have an investigative counselling and advisory role. He or she investigates ethical matters and advises on potential problem areas.
● no-one is obliged to discuss matters with the ombudsperson – employees can request help or advice on their own initiative if they feel they need it
● an ombudsperson must be independent, trusted by both management and employees. Confidentiality is also essential for the position to be effective
● an ombudsperson needs experience within the company – the position is suitable for an older respected employee who has assimilated the corporate value system. The position is appropriate for someone approaching retirement or a 'plateaued employee'.

● *An ethics committee*
MacDonald & Zepp point to Motorola as a company which has experimented successfully with this concept. They suggest: 'Committee membership should be rotated among employees thereby exposing them to the ethical problems submitted by either employees or managers.' These committees normally deal with policy making rather than specific complaints or unethical

actions. Committee decisions can then be used as firm clear guidelines for future action. According to MacDonald and Zepp, these committees are more popular in US businesses than ethical ombudspersons.

Codes of practice

Appendix 3 contains examples of a number of companies' codes of practice, both at a broad level, to cover all aspects of the business, and in specific areas of their activities.

Appendix 1: Ethical investment

The Merlin Ecology Fund is one of a number of investment funds, established in recent years, which deliberately invests only in the shares of companies that meet social responsibility criteria. It explains the origins of ethical investment in this way:

> 'The idea of assessing the behaviour of companies before investing in them began in the United States in the wake of the Vietnam War. Many individuals were shocked to find that their shareholdings in chemical companies had effectively made possible an event to which they were personally opposed.... Many of us are causing, albeit unwittingly, serious damage to our planet by investing in companies, which are harming the environment and failing in their responsibilities as corporate citizens. By taking care as investors to select companies with sound environmental and social management we can profit from our part in shaping a better world.'

> 'In 1987, the World Commission on Environment and Development assessed the role that industry must play in creating growth which is forceful as well as socially and environmentally sustainable. It stressed that industrialists must look for development solutions which are more in harmony with the natural order.'

In general, ethical investment trusts tend to outperform trusts based on more traditional selection criteria. For example, Friends Provident Stewardship Trust, dating from 1984, has consistently exceeded the average for UK Growth funds. Over five years to July 1 1989, its units grew by 178% compared with an average of 162%; over three years, by 50% against an average of 45%. 'I would not claim you would automatically do better with ethical investment, but it is helpful', Peter Sylvester, investment director of the trust told the *Sunday Times* in July 1989.

The criteria used by ethical investment trusts to select the companies they invest in vary, but will normally include:

- the financial track record
- research procedures (e.g. to ensure it is not carrying out unnecessary tests on animals)
- sales (to ensure that it has no military trade links)
- product processes (to ensure that it uses best available technology in terms of energy conservation and pollution controls and is environmentally aware)
- management policies
- personnel policies
- trading links and subsidaries in countries where human rights issues are significant
- community involvement policies

Companies which meet all these criteria may still not be well-managed. Some ethical trusts in the United States, for example, were depressed in value when Control Data, for years one of the flag-bearers of social responsibility and community action, fell into serious financial decline. In general, however, companies with good social responsibility records tend to be sensitive to what is going on in the world around them and willing to conform to – or lead, if the occasion arises – emerging societal concerns. Because they react more quickly to these issues, they are better prepared to take market advantage of the opportunities, which change opens up. This sensitivity to the broad environment is not limited to social responsibility issues; it covers many aspects of the business and is a significant factor in innovation and organizational dynamism.

Case study: *Merlin Ecology Fund*

The central principle of the Merlin Ecology Fund is concern for the environment. The managers will invest worldwide in a broad range of sectors. In considering companies within each sector, they will select those which are contributing the most to environmental protection.

However, to choose investments only in those industrial sectors which by their nature are environmentally harmless would be pointless, as the founders of the fund point out: 'Our aim is to identify the new industrial pioneers who marry sound environmental management and good business practice.'

The Fund's assessment areas cover four broad sectors:

- product process
- manufacturing process
- management policies
- corporate track record

The Fund's literature states: 'Companies are also reviewed against various social criteria which themselves have significant effects on the environment. Employees with low morale, for instance, are less likely to care about their work and its pollution consequences. Policies on animal testing, attitudes to women, minorities, the community and waste management are strong indicators of the sense of moral responsibility felt by a compnay. Many of the most successful have just this sense of social commitment and on this basis, investing according to one's principles can be sound too.'

The fund will not invest in any company directly concerned with South Africa, armaments, nuclear power or the tobacco industries. At the same time, the fund managers will make no investment in a company unless they are convinced that it has the prospects for capital appreciation and the capacity to pay a secure dividend.

Among Merlin's portfolio favourites is Fuel Tech, a company with a leading technology for the prevention of acid rain. It explains why:

'In Europe and US alone, 20 million tonnes of NOx are emitted from power stations and industrial boilers. Fuel Tech's NOx-out process is the most cost effective solution to the removal of these emissions. In 1988, the largest German utility company, RWE, accepted a Fuel Tech installation at one of its boilers. Results exceeded expectations. '

The German deadline for emission reduction was in late 1989 and Fuel Tech technology offered the best available process to reduce the pollution within that time.

Case study: *Quaker Oats*

Quaker is one of the fund's featured companies, for the following reasons:

'In Autumn 1988, the US corn harvest was afflicted with a potent carcinogen fungus, aflatoxin. The number-one-ready-to-eat-cereal producer went to extraordinary lengths to stop aflatoxin from creeping into its breakfast cereal and other foodstuffs. It set a limit of 15 parts aflatoxin per billion, a standard 25% more exacting than the federal government's guidelines.

Quaker Oats also maintains a solid and dependable reputation in the food, pet foods, children's toys (Fisher Price) and retail store sectors.

Quaker has a profit sharing plan with more than 63% of its US employees stockholders. It has a long history of recruiting women for professional and executive positions. Environmentally, there is a division with overall responsibility for environmental management, industrial hygiene and safety. In addition Environmental audits are carried out.

Food related wastes are recycled and made into animal feedstock, oils and greases are used again and the company prides itself in its water analyses and treatment before and after use.

The company donates over one per cent of its pre-tax earnings to charitable causes.'

Checklist
1. Is your company included in the portfolio of any ethical investment trusts?
2. What would you have to do to get it included?

Appendix 2: The survey of social responsibility performance

As part of the research for this guide, we sent questionnaires to 800 companies which were known to have an interest in social responsibility programmes. About 80 responded with information and 42 completed the detailed questionnaire. Their responses provide a valuable insight into the organization of social responsibility activities within British companies today. Almost all the companies were of large or medium size and they covered most major sectors of industry and commerce.

All of the companies had some relevant activities, but only 71% had a department or individual with specific responsibility for social responsibility issues. In all but 2 of those that did have such a person or department, it reported to someone at board level.

Slightly more than half had a specific strategy for enhancing the organization's social responsibility performance and these companies tended to have a broader spread of activities.

Allocation of funds to social responsibility activities most frequently takes place at board level (59%) and/or through a public affairs or social responsibility department (55%). Only 12% handle all or part of their giving through staff committees.

We asked companies to identify in which areas of social responsibility they maintained guidelines or policies. The results indicate considerable variation in areas of concern – some are clearly higher priority than others. Among the most common areas for formal guidelines were:
- a general statement of business ethics: only 7% did not have one and 55% had such policies at both corporate and divisional level
- fair trading, fair marketing, product safety and service: again, many companies had guidelines at both corporate and divisional levels. The surprise here was that a quarter of companies did not have policies in these areas at all. Moreover, less than half had programmes to ensure fair trading or fair marketing, while only just over half had programmes of product safety. Service, clearly now in vogue, fared better, with 78% saying they had defined

programmes of activities to promote and improve it
- equal opportunities: 95% had policies here; however, only 64% had a programme of activities to promote equal opportunity
- health and safety: 98% had guidelines, but only 81% had programmes to put them into effect
- employment security: 71% companies said they had policies here, with the majority of these taking active steps to ensure they fulfilled the commitments made
- pollution prevention: 78% had guidelines, but only 52% had programmes to implement them
- education and schools liaison: 88% had guidelines; 60% had active programmes
- purchasing ethics: 69% had guidelines; less than half had a programme to support them.

The picture that emerges is one of good intentions often unfulfilled.

A variety of other areas were seen as worthy of guidelines by only a minority of respondents. Only 21% had any sort of policy to encourage whistleblowing (encouraging employees to register dissent when they believe the company is acting unethically or illegally). Rather more (50%) had policies on lobbying, but a mere 21% felt it necessary to spell out their views on human rights issues.

In general, the companies tended to be rather lukewarm about energy usage, with 64% having a policy and less than half doing anything about it. The use of non-renewable resources and urban renewal drew even less interest.

Interest in sponsoring the Arts and research was also less common than might have been expected. 60% of companies reported that they had guidelines covering these areas; however, only 36% gave active support.

When asked whether they had a budget and annual expenditure plan for social responsibility, 67% said they had one at corporate level; 45% at divisional level. One company in four had no budget or expenditure plan at all and one organization said that it simply set an overall public relations budget, from which spending on social responsibility issues was funded. However, the great majority of companies are spending more in real terms on social responsibility issues than they were five years ago. The main reasons they gave were :
- increased need to preserve and enhance the corporate image (71%)
- longstanding corporate philosophy (57%)

- support of marketing activities (50%)

Pressure from employees, the general public and competition had been significantly less influential in causing increased spending (at 17%, 19% and 14% respectively); pressure from investors (contrary to many pundits) of much less again, at 5%. Only one company had been driven to increase spending as a result of a major PR disaster.

Next, we examined the areas where the responding companies expected to increase their level of activity. The most common responses were education and schools liaison, at 71%, and pollution prevention at 67%, a massive growth of interest in both cases. Close behind, at 62%, 62% and 50% respectively, and reflecting a similar upsurge in interest, were energy usage, health and safety, and use of non-renewable resources.

Only a minority of companies intend to increase their spending on the Arts (26%), or on sponsored research (29%), or on seeding community initiatives, such as those to assist crime prevention, tackle homelessness or encourage small businesses (36%). Similar proportions plan to become more involved in lobbying, and in providing employment security. At the bottom of the pile, only two companies aim to become more active in the area of human rights, only six aim to pay more attention to the issue of whistle-blowing and only seven intend to upgrade their purchasing or marketing ethics.

These responses tend to support the companies' statements about why they are increasing social responsibility spending. If social responsibility activities are viewed primarily as responses to marketing and image-building needs, it is inevitable that they will follow current fashions in media and government attention. The strong interest in education and schools liaison, however, presumably also involves an element of concern to secure an adequate labour pool among young people as demographic changes bite.

The dominance of self-interest (albeit enlightened) over community interest is indicated by the fact that only 24% claim to have made decisions on social responsibility grounds against direct commercial interests.

The majority of companies (83%) also perceive that they are far from alone in becoming more conscious of their social responsibilities. A slightly lower percentage (71%) say that British companies in general are responding to those responsibilities. However, very few of the respondents make the effort to exchange information frequently with other companies, to identify best practice in social responsibility; indeed 55% say they do so rarely or never.

These organizations are rather less unanimous when it comes to defining the most significant challenges that face those responsible for social responsibility, in doing their jobs. Lack of cash is the most common restraint (36%) followed by getting the organization's views across to pressure groups (31%), lack of employee involvement (19%) and lack of top management commitment (19%).

Only 5% felt that the quality of community projects on offer was a serious problem, but there was a sharp divide (40% vs. 43%) over how well community groups and charities generally positioned themselves to receive aid.

Summary of conclusions
Companies in Britain are generally increasing in awareness and activity in social responsibility, but tend to limit their involvement to a relatively narrow range of issues. Although most have a formal structure to manage social responsibility, the lack of a social responsibility strategy in about half of these organizations raises questions about their effectiveness in achieving business and/or community goals. The failure by so many organizations to seek out best practice elsewhere suggests a lack of commitment to managing this aspect of corporate endeavour as rigorously as the commercial activities, which it ultimately underpins.

Social responsibility in British business

A survey by the ITEM Research Unit

1. Does your company have an individual or a department, which is responsible for social responsibility issues either full time or as part of their job description?
   Yes ....   No ....

1a. Who do they/it report to? ....

2. Do you have a specific strategy for enhancing your organisation's social responsibility performance?
   Yes ....   No ....

3. Do you have any specific guidelines on the following issues? Please tick as appropriate.

	At corporate level	At divisional/ local level
– General business ethics	....	....
– Responsibilities towards customers		
e.g. – fair trading practices	....	....
– fair marketing practices	....	....
– product safety	....	....
– service	....	....
– other (please specify)		
– Responsibilities towards employees		
e.g. – equal opportunities	....	....
– health and safety	....	....
– developing talent	....	....
– employment security	....	....
– whistleblowing	....	....
– other (please specify)		
– Responsibilities towards suppliers		
e.g. – purchasing ethics	....	....
– other (please specify)		
– Responsibilities towards the political arena		
e.g. lobbying	....	....
– third world issues	....	....
– human rights	....	....
– other (please specify)		
– Responsibilities towards the broader community		
e.g. – education and schools liaison	....	....
– the Arts	....	....
– research	....	....
– seeding community initiatives (e.g. crime prevention, health, homelessness, small business)	....	....
– other (please specify)		
– Responsibilities towards the environment		
e.g. – pollution	....	....
– energy usage	....	....
– use of non-renewable resources	....	....
– urban renewal	....	....
– other (please specify)		

4. Do you have a budget and annual expenditure plan for social responsibility projects?

4a. At corporate level?   4b. At divisional/local level?
Yes ....   No ....   Yes ....   No ....

5. Do you have a defined programme of activities in the following areas? Please tick as appropriate.

	At corporate level	At divisional/ local level
− Responsibilities towards customers		
e.g. − fair trading practices	....	....
− fair marketing practices	....	....
− product safety	....	....
− service	....	....
− other (please specify)		
− Responsibilities towards employees		
e.g. − equal opportunities	....	....
− health and safety	....	....
− developing talent	....	....
− employment security	....	....
− whistleblowing	....	....
− other (please specify)		
− Responsibilities towards suppliers		
e.g. − purchasing ethics	....	....
− other (please specify)		
− Responsibilities towards the political arena		
e.g. − lobbying	....	....
− third world issues	....	....
− human rights	....	....
− other (please specify)		
− Responsibilities towards the broader community		
e.g. − education and schools liaison	....	....
− the Arts	....	....
− research	....	....
− seeding community initiatives (e.g. crime prevention, health, homelessness, small business)	....	....
− other (please specify)		

	At corporate level	At divisional/ local level
– Responsibilities towards the environment		
e.g. – pollution	....	....
– energy usage	....	....
– use of non-renewable resources	....	....
– urban renewal	....	....
– other (please specify)		

We would appreciate details of as many of these as possible for inclusion in the book.

6. Are you spending more than five years ago in real terms on social responsibility issues? Yes .... No ....
   If so, what have been the main reasons for doing so? Please tick as appropriate.
   - increased need to preserve and enhance corporate image? ....
   - support of marketing activities? ....
   - pressure from the general public? ....
   - competitive pressure? ....
   - longstanding corporate philosophy? ....
   - recovery from a major PR disaster? ....
   - other (please specify)

7. Do you expect your level of activity in the field of social responsibility to increase? In which areas?
   - Responsibilities towards customers
   e.g. – fair trading practices ....
   – fair marketing practices ....
   – product safety ....
   – service ....
   – other (please specify)

   – Responsibilities towards employees
   e.g. – equal opportunities ....
   – health and safety ....
   – developing talent ....
   – employment security ....
   – whistleblowing ....
   – other (please specify)

   – Responsibilities towards suppliers
   e.g. – purchasing ethics ....
   – other (please specify)

– Responsibilities towards the political arena
e.g. – lobbying   ....
    – third world issues   ....
    – human rights   ....
    – other (please specify)

– Responsibilities towards the broader community
e.g. – education and schools liaison
    – the arts   ....
    – research   ....
    – seeding community initiatives   ....
     (e.g. crime prevention, health, homelessness, small business)
    – other (please specify)   ....

– Responsibilities towards the environment
e.g. – pollution   ....
    – energy usage   ....
    – use of non-renewable resources   ....
    – urban renewal   ....
    – other (please specify)

8. What do you consider to be the most significant challenges facing those responsible for social responsibility issues in doing their job?
   – never enough cash?   ....
   – lack of top management commitment?   ....
   – getting the organisation's view across to pressure groups?   ....
   – lack of employee involvement?   ....
   – the low quality of community projects on offer?   ....
   – others (please specify)

9. Do you share information on social responsibility with other companies?
   – frequently?   ....
   – occasionally?   ....
   – rarely or never?   ....

10. How do you allocate funds?
    – at board level or at board committee level?   ....
    – through a public affairs department/social responsibility department?   ....
    – through a staff committee?   ....
    – other (please specify)

11. Has your company ever made decisions on socially responsible grounds against its direct commercial interests? If yes, please give examples overleaf or on a separate enclosure.
    Yes ....   No ....

12. Do you feel that community groups and charities in general position themselves well to receive aid?
    Yes ....   No ....

13. Do you consider that British companies in general are becoming more conscious of their social responsibilities?
    Yes ....   No ....
    And are they responding to these needs?
    Yes ....   No ....

    If you have any particularly innovative projects in their field, please could you give us details for inclusion in the book.
    Your name ....   Your company ....
    Your job title ....   Telephone ....
                                             Facsimile ....
    RETURN TO: ITEM Research, Burnham House, Burnham, Bucks SL1 7JZ

Appendix 3: Codes of practice

'The process of drawing up codes and keeping them up-to-date can clarify issues, concentrate minds and build a common commitment. Their promulgation sets norms and standards against which lapses can be admitted and behaviour changed. Moreover, a corporate culture can then be more easily sustained by internal social pressures whereas, with nothing written, the informal cultures that develop are very difficult to deal with,' writes Neville Cooper, chairman of the The Top Management Partnership and chairman of the Institute of Business Ethics in an occasional paper 'What's all this about Business Ethics?'

In another booklet 'Company Philosophies and Codes of Business Ethics', also published by the institute, writer and researcher, Simon Webley outlines a model code and gives advice on how to set about drawing it up.

He says that the statement and code should not be left to an enthusiast on the board or delegated to the personnel department. In practice, he maintains, companies which value their statements and make use of them in daily life involve the most senior officers in drawing up and publishing them.

Guidelines to a model code of business principles
1. Preface or introduction (signed by the chairman, chief executive officer or both).

Start with a sentence on the purpose of the statement. Mention the values which are important to the top management in the conduct of the business such as integrity, efficiency, professionalism and responsibility.

Set out the role of the company in the community and end with a personal endorsement of the statement and the expectation that the standards set in it will be maintained by all involved in the organisation.

Date the preface.
2. Include:

a. The object of the business
The service which is being provided and the business's role in society as the company sees it.
b. Customer relations
The importance of customer satisfaction and good faith in all agreements. The priority given to customer needs, fair pricing and after sales service.
c. Shareholders or other providers of money
The protection of investment made in the company and proper return on money lent. A commitment to effective communication with this group of people.
d. Suppliers
Long term co-operation. Prompt settling of bills. Joint actions to achieve quality and efficiency.
e. Employees
How the business values employees. The company's policies towards recruitment, development and training, rewards, communication, work conditions, health and safety, industrial relations, equal employment opportunity, retirement, severance and redundancy.
f. The wider community
Compliance with the spirit as well as the letter of the law. The company's obligation to conform to the environmental and safety standards. The involvement of the company and its staff in local affairs. The corporate policy on giving to education and charities. The leadership role of the business in maintaining high standards both within the organization and in its dealings with others.
g. Other matters
Relations with competitors, research and development policy and management responsibility. The ethical standards expected of employees.

The issue of ethical standards is often best expanded in a separate statement addressed primarily at staff, says Webley, who suggests that a typical, effective version will be short and written in simple language. It should be concerned with problems experienced by employees and include something about procedures to be followed when confronted with an ethical dilemma. It should also make clear what will happen if the code is breached.

1. Introduction
This should state the reason why the code has been produced. It should state that it applies to everyone and that anyone found breaching it will be subject to serious disciplinary action.

2. Conflicts of interest

A clause covering conflicts of interest – for example, in the company's dealings with immediate members of the employee's family. A directive that all potential conflicts should be reported to their immediate superior and recorded. A ban on share dealing with information obtained while working.

3. Giving and receiving gifts

The code must contain guidance on giving and receiving cash, services, hospitality or bribes in any form. It should include a statement that all offers made as an inducement should be refused.

State company policy on giving gifts to others.

State that any gifts received must be reported to a superior and recorded. The fact that business entertainment should be on a reciprocal basis and on a scale consistent with the status of the employee within the organisation.

4. Confidentiality

A statement that all information obtained during work is the property of the company.

State that confidential information must not be disclosed to unauthorised person and that this also applies when the employee has left the company.

Advise of steps to be taken to safeguard information that might be useful to competitors.

5. Environment

Standard for the working environment and the effect of business activity on local communities. A statement that the health and safety of employees is paramount. State that staff are required to see that products and operations not only comply with legal requirements but take into account the well-being of the general public – especially those living in the general vicinity of manufacturing plants.

6. Equal opportunity

An undertaking that selections for posts shall be based only on suitability. State that there will be no discrimination on the grounds of race, religion, marital status, colour, nationality, disability or ethnic or national origin. Outline similar undertakings on promotion and security of employment.

7. Other areas

There are a number of other areas that might be covered in such a code.

These include

– political activities
– obligations under competition or anti-trust laws
– moonlighting by employees
– sexual harassment.

The role of the social responsibility audit

Our research uncovered a number of companies, which had – usually fairly recently – instituted enviornmental audits, customer service audits and audits of specialist issues, such as equal opportunities in hiring and promotion. We did not find any company, however, which undertook a comprehensive audit of all the activities which could be grouped under the heading of social responsibility.

The problem for the concerned company is that, while it is busy tackling perceived priority issues, matters may be going seriously awry in areas which are not subjected to senior management analysis and scrutiny.

We believe strongly that the social auditing process should be as broad as possible, to protect the organization from as wide a variety of potential problems as possible.

So what is a social responsibility audit and how does it work?

In principle an SR audit is like any other business audit. It attempts to answer the management need for information on where the organization's performance is now, and where it ought to be.

Normally, an audit will operate at three levels:

1) policy:
– are there written policies for each area of social responsibility?
– do they reflect current thinking/knowledge?
– do people within the relevant parts of the organization know that the policies exist and roughly what they say?

2) systems and standards for measuring performance in each area:
– do the systems exist?
– do they measure the right things?
– do they work?/are they used?
– are the standards high enough? (i.e. will they be overtaken by

legislation?) can we seize competitive advantage by achieving higher standards? how do our standards compare with best practice elsewhere?
– are the standards clearly understandable and precise enough to be measured accurately, year on year?

3) recording and analysing performance
– current
– versus previous years'
– versus targets set.

In practice, initial audits are likely to discover that the necessary measurement systems do not exist. In many ways, the SR auditor is then in a similar situation to the financial auditor, who finds that there is no system to record invoices.

   In those circumstances, he or she can:
• record the existence of active programmes and specific achievements within them
• recommend where the company should develop systems and standards and what these should contain.

Every area of social responsibility can be measured in this way. To give some examples:
• equal opportunities
– % of workforce as total and % at different levels from each minority group
• pollution control
– parts per million of emissions
• raw materials purchase (e.g. tropical hardwoods)
– what steps could the company reasonably take? How many of these (%) has it taken?
• customer service
– measurement of service quality by questionnaire or focus groups
– complaints
– repeat business
• supplier issues
– attitude surveys
– level of contact/sharing
and so on.

Finally, an SR audit will seek to examine the degree of involvement and commitment to social responsibility at various levels in the organization. For example:
• top management only

- the management group as a whole
- all employees
- all employees plus some suppliers and customers

This information, once analysed, has two main uses. Firstly, it helps the company establish a coherent social responsibility plan – a framework of activities that meet the needs of its various SR policies.

Secondly, it provides an excellent public relations platform, particularly if the company can point to continuing improvements both in standards aimed at and in actual performance. These issues are of interest to all stakeholders, but particularly to the employees, for whom pride in their employing organization is an important part of motivation.

We recommend that, at the minimum, companies publish the results of a SR audit in their company newspaper. More ambitiously, they should consider publishing a separate social audit report to accompany the annual financial report and accounts.

Examples of codes of practice

The following examples have been chosen to illustrate some of the variety of statements, which organizations have used to establish ethical values and principles within their organizations.

Case study: *Trusthouse Forte plc*

Trusthouse Forte plc has opted for a short written outline of company philosophy. It states:

The Company Philosophy
- To increase profitability and earnings per share each year in order to encourage investment and to improve and expand the business
- To give complete customer satisfaction by efficient and courteous service and value for money
- To support managers and their staff in using personal initiative to improve the profit and quality of their operations while observing company policies
- To provide good working conditions and to maintain effective communications at all levels to develop better understanding and assist decision making
- To ensure no discrimination against sex, race, colour or creed and to train, develop and encourage promotion within the company based on merit and ability

● To act with integrity at all times and to maintain a proper sense of responsibility towards the public

● To recognise the importance of each and every employee who contributes towards these aims.

Case study: *The Body Shop*

The Body Shop Charter
We declare that:
1. The Body Shop's goals and values are as important as our products and our profits
2. Our policies and our products are geared to meet the real people, both inside and outside the company
3. Honesty, integrity and caring form the foundations of the company, and should flow through everything we do
4. We care about each other as individuals: we will continue to endeavour to bring meaning and pleasure to the workplace
5. We care about our customers, and will continue to bring humanity into the market place
6. We care about humanizing the business community: we will continue to show that success and profits can go in hand with ideals and values.

In addition the Body Shop declares:
● We will demonstrate our care for the world in which we live, by respecting fellow human beings, by not harming animals, by working to conserve our planet

● We will continue to create products which show that we care: by not testing on animals, by using naturally-based ingredients that are close to source, by making products which work for our customers

● We will continue to search, to challenge, to question, to celebrate life and generate joy and excitement

● We embrace everyone who works for The Body Shop and with The Body Shop as part of our extended family. We are all the company: it is up to us to make it work.

Case study: *Royal Dutch/Shell Group of Companies*

The Royal Dutch/Shell Group of Companies has a general statement of business principles which was published in the Institute of Business Ethics booklet 'Company Philosophies and Codes of Practice'. In the introduction to the detailed statement, the chairman of the Committee of Managing Directors of the Service Companies, Mr L. C. van Wachem, explains why such a document is important. He says: 'The group is typified by decentralized, highly diversified and widespread operations, in which operating companies are given wide freedom of action. However, the upholding of the Shell reputation is a common bond which can be maintained only by honesty and integrity in all activities. A single failure, whether it be wilful or due to a misplaced zeal, or short term expediency, can have very serious effects on the group as a whole'.

Statement of General Business Principles

1. Objectives
The objectives of Shell companies are to engage efficiently, responsibly and profitably in the oil, gas, chemicals, coal, metals and selected other businesses, and to play an active role in the search for and development of other sources of energy. Shell companies seek a high standard of performance and aim to maintain a long term position in their respective competitive environments.

2. Responsibilities
Four areas of responsibility are recognised:
a. To shareholders
To protect shareholders' investment and provide an acceptable return.
b. To employees
To provide all employees with good and safe conditions of work, good and competitive terms and conditions of service; to promote the development and best use of human talent and equal opportunity development; and to encourage the involvement of employees in the planning and direction of their work, recognising that success depends on the full contribution of all employees.
c. To customers
To develop and provide products and services which offer value in terms of price and quality, supported by the requisite technological and commercial expertise. There is no guaranteed future: Shell companies depend on winning and maintaining customers' support.
d. To society
To conduct business as responsible corporate members of society, observing applicable laws of countries in which they operate, giving due regard to safety and environmental standards and societal aspirations.
   These four areas of responsibility can be seen as an inseparable whole.

3. Economic Principles
Profitability is essential to discharging these responsibilities and staying in business. It is a measure both of efficiency and of the ultimate value that people place on Shell products and services.
   It is essential to the proper allocation of corporate resources and necessary to support the continuing investment required to develop and produce future energy supplies to meet consumer needs. Without profits and a

strong financial foundation it would not be possible to fulfil the responsibilities outlined above.

Shell companies work in a wide variety of social, political and economic
environments over the nature of which they have little influence, but in
general they believe that the interests of the community can be served
most efficiently by a market economy.

Criteria for investment decisions are essentially economic but also take
into account social and environmental considerations and an appraisal
of the security of the investment.

4. Voluntary Codes of Conduct

Policies of Shell companies are consistent with the two existing inter-
nationally agreed voluntary codes of conduct for multinational enterprises, the OECD Declaration and Guidelines for International Investment
and Multinational Enterprises and the ILO Tripartite Declartion of Principles.

5. Business Integrity

Shell companies insist on honesty and integrity in all aspects of their
business. All employees are required to avoid conflicts of interest between
their private financial activities and their part in the conduct of company
business. The offer, payment, soliciting and acceptance of bribes in any
form are unacceptable practices. All transactions on behalf of a Shell
company must be appropriately described in the accounts of the company
in accordanbce with established procedures and subject to audit.

6. Political Activities

a. Shell companies endeavour always to act commercially, operating
within existing national laws in a socially responsible manner, abstaining
from participation in party politics. It is, however, their legitimate right
and responsibility to speak out on matters that affect the interests of
employees, customers and shareholders, and on matters of general interest, where they have a contribution to make that is based on particular
knowledge.

b. Political payments

As a policy Shell companies do not make payments to political parties,
organizations or their representatives.

c. Employees

Where employees, in their capacity as citizens, wish to engage in activities
in the community, including standing for election to public office, favourable consideration is given to their being enabled to do so, where this is
appropriate in the light of local circumstances.

7. Environment

It is the policy of Shell companies to conduct their activities in such a way as to take foremost account of the health and safety of their employees and of other persons, and to give proper regard to the conservation of the environment. In implementing this policy Shell companies not only comply with the requirements of the relevant legislation but promote in an appropriate manner measures for the protection of health, safety and the environment for all who may be affected directly or indirectly by their activities. Such measures pertain to safety of operations carried out by employees and contractors; product safety, prevention of air, water and soil pollution; and precautions to minimize damage from such accidents as may nevertheless occur.

8. Grants and General Community Projects

The most important contribution that companies can make to the social and material progress of the countries in which they operate is in performing their basic activities as efficiently as possible. In addition the need is recognised to take a constructive interest in societal matters which may not be directly related to the business. Opportunities for involvement, for example, through community, educational or donations programmes, will vary depending upon the size of the company concerned, the nature of the local society and the scope for useful private initiatives.

9. Information

The importance of the activities in which Shell companies are engaged and their impact on national economies and individuals are well recognised. Full relevant information about these activities is therefore provided to legitimately interested parties, both national and international, subject to any overriding consideration of confidentiality proper to the protection of the business and the interests of third parties and the need to avoid wasteful information exercises.

Increasingly the behaviour of large companies is subject to rigorous external scrutiny. The reputation of the Royal Dutch/Shell Group of Companies depends on the existence and acknowledgement of clearly understood principles and responsibilities and their observance in day to day practice in widely differing environments. Although individual operating companies may elaborate their own statements to meet their national situations, this statment of general business principles serves as a basis on which companies of the Royal Dutch/Shell Group, in their operations, pursue the highest standards of busines behaviour. Shell companies also promote the application of these principles in joint ventures in which they participate.

Code of conduct for employees of British Gas plc

1. Financial or other interest
a) Conflict of interest
Anyone who has a personal interest in an organisation with which British Gas has or may have a business relationship is vulnerable to allegations of impropriety. If a personal interest or that of a member of one's immediate family might influence the company's business relationship, it should be formally declared in writing at the HQ to the company secretary or in a region to the regional secretary, who will record the declaration of interest in a register maintained for this purpose. Examples of personal interest that should be declared are a directorship, a large share-holding, promise of future employment or the employment of a close relative or friend in a position of influence in an organisation which may be given business or awarded contracts by the company.
b) Dealing in shares of British Gas plc
Some staff have access during their work to unpublished infor-mation about the company's activities or future prospects which, if published, might affect the share prices. If you are in this special position and you wish to buy or sell British Gas shares, you must first study the separate guidelines on share dealing which will be available from your head of department.
c) Dealing in shares of other companies
You should not deal in the securities of any company when, by virtue of your position as an employee of British Gas, you are in possession of information likely upon publication to affect the market price of those securities. This includes shares or debentures or options to subscribe for shares or debentures.
d) Purchasing and supplies department
In addition to the foregoing, if you are a senior officer or above within the purchasing department at headquarters or in a region, you will be required from time to time formally to decalre in writing to your HQ or regional director or controller details of any shareholding, involvement or activity which could give rise to a conflict of interest. Everyone employed in the industry's purchasing function is expected to abide by the Institute of Pur-chasing and Supply's Code of Ethics.
e) Declaration of interest
In addition to the foregoing, if in any other department you are in a position to influence the choice of contractors or suppliers, you may be required to make a similiar declaration at the discretion of

your managing director, HQ director or regional chairman as appropriate.

2. Gifts, hospitality or benefits

It is a criminal offence to accept or solicit any gift or consideration from anyone as an inducement or reward for showing favour in connection with the company's business.

To avoid any possibility of misunderstanding, all such offers should be politely but firmly declined. Gifts delivered should be returned to the sender with an appropriately worded letter and the matter reported to your superior. The only exception is that gifts of a trifling nature such as calendars or diaries may be accepted.

Any approaches from contractors, suppliers or traders, seeking favoured treatment in consideration of any offers of benefits or hospitality must be firmly declined and the circumstances reported to your superior.

Business entertainment should be on a reciprocal basis and on a scale consistent with that which you, when host, would be authorised to arrange.

If you have the slightest doubt about accepting any offer of benefits or hospitality you have clearly recognised a potentially dangerous situation and should seek guidance from your superior.

3. Confidentiality of information

We all have a responsibilty to safeguard the confidentiality of any information acquired during the course of our work, including information kept on computers and a duty never to use it for personal advantage. Such information should not be disclosed outside. Equally, we should all be on our guard and avoid careless and thoughtless talk which may damage the company's business or that of any of its customers.

4. Confidential disclosures

Any disclosure or similiar communication made to management in accordance with this code will be treated as confidential although it may be discussed with your director or controller.

If in doubt

This code has been prepared to give guidance. If you are ever in any doubt about any matter concerning conduct, you should seek advice from your superior. You should also be aware that breaches of the code can result in diciplinary action.
b) Examples of codes of practice in specific areas

i) A Model Code for Customers
The Kwik-Fit Group's mission statement on customers

Kwik Fit's customer care philosophy derives from a mission statement published by founder and chairman, Tom Farmer in 1972.

'At Kwik-Fit the most important person is the customer and it must be the aim of all of us to give 100% satisfaction 100% of the time. Our continued success depends on the loyalty of our customers. We are committed to a policy of offering them the best value for money with a fast, courteous and professional service. We offer the highest quality products and guarantees. We at Kwik-Fit recognise that our people are our most valuable asset. The manager and his fitters at our centres are the all-important contact with the customers and they are the key to the success of the Kwik-Fit Group.'

ii) A Model Statement on Equal Opportunities
Ford Motor Company's joint statement on equal opportunity

Ford Motor Company hands out the following statement, written in November 1988 to all employees.

Signed by the company and its trade unions, entitled 'Joint Statement on Equal Opportunity', it is one of the most comprehensive equal opportunities policy documents in the country:

1. Commitment to Equal Opportunity

1.1 The company and the trade unions are committed to the principle of equal opportunity in employment. The company and the trade unions declare their opposition to any form of less favourable treatment, whether through direct or indirect discrimination, accorded to employees and applicants for employment on the grounds of race, religious creed, colour, nationality, ethnic or national origins, marital status or sex.

1.2 The company and the trade unions similarly declare their opposition to any form of less favourable treatment accorded to employees and applicants for employment on the grounds of non-job related handicaps and unfair discrimination on the grounds of age.

1.3 The company and trade unions recognise their obligations under the Sex Discrimination Act 1975 and the Race Relations Act 1976 and support the spirit and intent of the related codes of practice:
– for the elimination of discrimination on the grounds of sex and marriage and the promotion of equality of opportunity in employment

– for the elimination of racial discrimination and the promotion of equality of opportunity in employment.

2. Employment Practices

2.1 The company and the trade unions state their wholehearted support for the principle and practice of equal opportunity and agree that it is the duty of all employees to accept their personal responsibility for fostering a fully integrated community at work by adhering to the principles of equal opportunity and maintaining racial harmony. The company, will, therefore, actively promote equal opportunity through the application of employment policies which will ensure that individuals receive treatment which is fair, equitable and consistent with their relevant aptitudes, potential, skills and abilities. The trade unions will seek to ensure that all members and representatives comply with these principles and practices.

2.2 The company will ensure that individuals are recruited and selected, promoted and treated on objective criteria having regard to relevant aptitudes, potential, skills and abilities. In particular, no applicant or employee will be placed at a disadvantage by the requirements or conditions which are not necessary to the performance of the job or which constitute indirect unfair discrimination.

2.3 The company and the trade unions recognise the problems that sexual harassment may cause in the workplace and are jointly committed to ensuring that such unacceptable behaviour does not take place. Sexual harassment includes unwanted physical contact; suggestive remarks or behaviour; compromising invitations; demands for sexual favours and similiar unwanted behaviour. Sexual harassment is regarded as unfair discriminatory conduct and will be dealt with in accordance with the procedures set out in 4.2 below.

3. Monitoring and Review Arrangements

3.1 The company and the trade unions recognise that regular monitoring of the ethnic origin and sex of employees is essential to the thorough review of the effectiveness of the joint statement and to this end the company will maintain and improve as necessary, the curent equal opportunity monitoring arrangments. These may be extended where agreed by the company and trade unions for the purpose of completing jointly agreed special exercises at local or national level.

3.2 The successful implementation of this joint statement is dependent on the regular examination of progress towards equal opportunity and the development of local initiatives. To this end, local management and trade unions are expected to set up appropraite joint bodies at plant or equivalent level.

3.3 The company will send a copy of the company-wide annual review of equal opportunity statistics to the trade unions.
3.4 The practical application of this joint statement will be subject to regular review at national level to ensure that it continues to be fully effective.

4. Grievance and Disciplinary Procedures

4.1 The company and trade unions will ensure that individual employees or groups of employees who believe that they have experienced direct or indirect unfair discrimination are properly represented. Any employee who feels that he or she has been treated unfairly in connection with his or her employment should raise his or her grievance through the appropriate procedure when every effort will be made to secure a satisfactory resolution. In addition, both the company and the trade unions will ensure that any employees making a complaint of unfair discrimination will be protected from victimization.
4.2 The company will continue to treat unfair disciminatory conduct by any employee as a disciplinary offence.

5. Training and Advertising

5.1 The company will provide in agreement with the trade unions, suitable and relevant equal oportunity training, as necessary and on a jointly agreed syllabus, for employees and trade union representatives. The trade unions agree to support and participate in such training programmes and to encourage their representatives to attend where appropriate. These arrangements in no way preclude the separate provision of training by the company or the trade unions to meet particular needs.
5.2 When vacancies are advertised, the company will continue to ensure such advertising, both in placement and content, is compatible with the terms of this joint statement. To this end, opportunities will be taken through language, images or declarations, as appropriate, to show that the company is an equal opportunity employer.

6. Communications

6.1 The company and the trade unions undertake to bring the principles set out above to the attention of all employees and the trade union representatives.

iii) A Code for the Environment

3M's Official Environment Policy

Under its worldwide environmental policy 3M will continue to recognise and exercise responsibility to:
– to solve its own environmental pollution and conservation problems
– prevent pollution at source wherever possible
– develop products that will have a minimum effect on the environment
– conserve natural resources through the use of reclamation and other appropriate methods
– assure that its facilities and products meet and sustain the regulations of all federal, state and local environmental agencies
– assist wherever possible, governmental agencies and official organizations engaged in environmental activities

Appendix 4: Useful addresses

For further information and help, contact:

Responsibility towards customers

Committee of Advertising
Practice (CAP)
Brook House
2–16 Torrington Place
London
WC1E 7HN
071 580 5555

Responsibilities towards employees

Health Education Authority
Hamilton House
Mabledon Place
WC1H 9TX
071 383 3833

Institute of Manpower Studies
Mantell Building
University of Sussex
Falmer
Brighton
BN1 9RF
0273 686751

Institute of Personnel
Management
IPM House
Camp Road
Wimbledon
London
SW19 4UW
081 946 9100

New Ways to Work,
309, Upper Street,
London N1 2TY

Social Audit and Public Interest
Research Centre
PO Box 111
London
NW1 8XG
071 586 7771

The Training Agency
(Department of Employment)
Moorfoot
Sheffield
S1 4PQ

Purchasing

Business in the Community (BiC)
227A City Road
London
EC1V 1LX
071 253 3716

Furniture Industry Research
Association
Maxwell Road
Stevenage
Hertfordshire

Better Made in Britain
39-40 St James Place
London SW1A 1NS
071-491-0458

Institute of Purchasing and
Supply
Easton House
Easton on the Hill
Stamford, Lincs
PE9 3NZ
0780 56777

Regain information:

Kirklees and Wakefield Chamber
of Commerce
Tel: 0484 423455

Small Business Unit,
Durham University,
Durham,
Co.Durham.
091-374-2000

*Responsibilities towards the
broader community*

Charity Commision
St Albans House
57-60 Haymarket
London
SW1Y 4QX

Education 2000
Garden City Corpoartion Offices
The Broadway
Letchworth Garden City
Hertfordshire
SG6 3AB

London Education Business
Partnership
c/o Whitbread & Co
The Brewery
Chiswell Street
London
EC1 4SD
071 606 4455

London Enterprise Agency
(LEntA)
4 Snow Hill
London
EC1A 2BS
071 236 3000

The Per Cent Club/ BiC
227A City Road
London EC1V 1LX
071 253 3716

*Responsiblities towards the
environment*

Business and the environment
Unit
Ian Oakins DTI
Room 1016, Ashdown House,
123 Victoria Street,
London SW1E 6RB
071 215 6082

Friends of the Earth,
26–28, Underwood Street,
London N1 7JQ
071 490 1555

Institute of Waste Management
(WM)
3 Albion Place
Northampton
NN1 1UD
0604 20426

Network for Environmental
Technology Transfer
Square de Meeus 25, B-1040,
Brussels
010 322 511 2462

Warren Spring Laboratory, DTI,
Gunnels Wood Road
Stevenage
Hertfordshire
SE1 2BX
Environmental enquiry point –
0800 585 794

International Institute for
Environment and Development
3 Endsleigh Street
London
WC1

Association of Environment
Conscious Builders
Windlake House
The Pump Field
Coaley
Gloucester GL11 5DX

Water Services Association of
England and Wales (information
on the water and sewage
businesses)
Queen Anne's Gate,
London
SW1H 9BT
071 222 8111

Worldwide Fund for Nature – UK
Panda House
Weyside Park
Godalming,
Surrey

How to organise

Allied Dunbar
Allied Dunbar Centre
Swindon
SN1 1EL
0793 514514

Social responsibility auditing

The ITEM Group
Burnham House,
High Street,
Burnham
Bucks SL1 7JZ

Confederation of British
Industry,
Centre Point,
103, Oxford Street,
London WC1A 1DU

Bibliography

Bellamy, David and Quayle, Brenda, The Tees, The Living River, David Bellamy Associates, 1988.

Campbell Brady, Ian, Enlightened Entrepreneurs, Weidenfeld and Nicolson, London 1987.

Clutterbuck, David, How to be a good corporate citizen – a manager's guide to making social responsibility work – and pay, McGraw Hill, Maidenhead, 1981.

CBI, PA Consulting Group, Waking up to a better environment, CBI, London, March 1990

CBI, Clean up it's good business, CBI booklet, July 1986.

Cooper, Neville, What's all this about business ethics – an occasional paper, Institute of Business Ethics, London, 1989.

Crabb, Stephen, Has industry seen the green light? article for Personnel Management magazine, April 1990.

Drummond, John and Carmichael, Sheena, Good Business – guide to corporate responsibility and business ethics, Business Books, June 1989

Midland Banks on a nursery for ex-staff, *Daily Telegraph* October 4, 1989.

Department of Trade and Industry, Cutting Your Losses – a business guide to waste minimisation, DTI, 1990.

Department of Trade and Industry, Your Business and The Environment – Protecting the environment: next steps for business, DTI, 1989.

Evans, Richard, The Times, Advertisers alerted over inaccurate environment claims, January 19, 1990.

Hampson, Chris, Industry and the environment – a question of balance, speech from the Cambridge lectures on Environment and Development 'Our Common Future', February 1989, booklet issued by ICI.

Hibbert, Vicky, Equal Opportunity Report, Equal Opportunity at Ford Motor Company, No 24, March/April 1989.

KPH Marketing, The Greener Employee, research study and report (1990)

Marek, Mayer, Environmental Ethics – the challenge for 3M, booklet published by 3M.

McDonald, Gael and Zepp, Raymond – What Should Be Done – a practical approach to business ethics, Management Decision 28,1 .

New Consumer magazine, Summer 1989

New Ways to Work Newsletter, Vol 5, No 4, 1989.

Producers with a conscience – Business in the community magazine, Business in the community, London 1989.

Sieff, Marcus (Lord Sieff of Brimpton), Don't ask the price, Weidenfeld and Nicolson, London 1986.

Sunday Times Magazine, Children of the New Revolution, March 1990

The Good Wood Guide – A Friends of the Earth Handbook, Friends of the Earth 1990

Webley, Simon, Company Philosophies and Codes of Business ethics – A guide to their drafting and use, Institute of Business Ethics, London, 1988.

World Commission on Environment and Development. Our Common Future. Oxford University Press, 1987.